RENEWALS 691-4574

CIVIL BLOOD

CIVIL BLOOD

Poems and Prose by

JILL BRECKENRIDGE

Engravings by R.W. Scholes

MILKWEED EDITIONS

CIVIL BLOOD
Poems and Prose by Jill Breckenridge
© 1986 by Jill Breckenridge
All rights reserved. Published 1986
Printed in the United States of America

89 88 87 86   5 4 3 2 1

Published by *Milkweed Editions*
an imprint of Milkweed Chronicle
Post Office Box 24303
Minneapolis, Minnesota 55424
Books may be ordered from the above address

Edited by Emilie Buchwald
Designed and Illustrated by R.W. Scholes © 1986

Library of Congress Card Number: 86-060097
ISBN: 0-915943-09-3 Paper
ISBN: 0-915943-10-7 Cloth

This publication is supported in part by grants provided by The First
Bank System Foundation; the Jerome Foundation; the Metropolitan
Regional Arts Council from funds appropriated by the Minnesota State
Legislature, and with special assistance from the McKnight Foundation;
and the United Arts Fund.

This book was written with funds and support from the Bush Foun-
dation, the Minnesota State Arts Board, and the Ragdale Foundation,
Lake Forest, Illinois.

Although the major events in this book are based on fact, many of the
characters and events are fictionalized.

For my aunt,
Josephine Breckenridge Paulson

FOREWORD

In *Civil Blood*, Jill Breckenridge tells stories, confronts history, surrounds us with characters, and haunts and transports us with voices like no other poet I have come across. This long poem about John Cabell Breckinridge, the statesman and Confederate general from Kentucky, about his family and others whose lives he touched directly or indirectly, is a stunning piece of work.

What we encounter here is an extraordinary marriage of fact and imagination, and an abundance of vision and skill which has led the poet to invent a kaleidoscope of voices, forms, styles and genres to create a panorama of the human heart that we associate only with rare, rich novels.

Yet Jill Breckenridge has done it in poetry. For this book wears its many years of research lightly; it is a *poem*, and astonishes the reader not so much with its facts, but with its language, the enormous range of it. There is a subtle use of musical principles operating in the arrangement of the book, but we needn't recognize this in order to admire the ease with which one voice gives way to a very different voice, to enjoy the surprise of finding a formally restrained poem next to a lyrical outburst, or a "document" or "true account" not far from a charming "folktale."

Each poem is appropriate for its speaker and occasion. We are disturbed by the facts of slavery, instructed in the realities of politics, moved by the destinies of people caught in the war—always within the context of characters who speak for all of us about the complex beings we are. The emphasis shifts properly from the overriding lyricism of Section I to narrative and reflection in Section II, which deals with the Civil War.

So often there is a touching authenticity and intimacy about the voices—"purity" is probably the most exact word; we are overhearing people speaking to themselves. Speakers need no rhetoric, since they are not attempting to persuade or impress anyone else. Here are two examples from the book's last section. First, Cabell, defeated and convinced that the Southern position was wrong, has returned home from exile.

He is looking at a horse in a field:

> In one pasture, an old trotter
>
> enjoys his retirement. I can't imagine
> a conscience as clear as his.

And in the last poem, Jacob, the former slave, now a freed-man being terrorized by the Ku Klux Klan, has begun to paint birds:

> The bird that God sends flies up
> in my mind and I catch it best I can.
>
> First a meadowlark — the yellow
> and stripes are stubborn
> to set down on the wood.
>
> Then I paint a crow, try to coax
> the blue out of the black. . . .

Jill Breckenridge coaxes every color of the spectrum out of a dark and stubborn time.

—Lisel Mueller

THE PEOPLE:

John Cabell Breckinridge — *lawyer, congressman, Vice President of the United States, Confederate general*
Laetitia — *Cabell's sister, one year younger*
Cabell's mother — *a recent widow*
Grandmother Black Cap — *Cabell's widowed grandmother*
John Breckinridge — *his grandfather, deceased*
Joseph Cabell Breckinridge — *his father, deceased*
Mary Breckinridge — *Cabell's wife*
Robert Breckinridge — *Cabell's uncle*
Jacob — *Cabell's personal slave*
Easter — *Jacob's sister*
Manda — *Jacob's mother*
Mr. Will — *the white overseer, Jacob's father*
Sam — *Jacob's grandfather*
Celia — *Jacob's grandmother, probably deceased*
Marcie — *Jacob's wife*
General Braxton Bragg — *Cabell's commander at the battle of Stones River in Tennessee*
Elise Bragg — *his wife*
Will Sommers — *farmer turned Confederate soldier*
Asa Lewis — *deserter who is executed; Will Sommers' best friend*
Tad Preston — *fourteen-year-old cadet conscripted from the Virginia Military Academy for boys*
Blue Ribbon Rosie — *camp follower*
General Jubal Early — *a Confederate general; Cabell's friend*
James and others in Sections III and IV — *Southerners after the war*

THE PLACES:

Cabell's Dale outside Lexington, Kentucky; Washington; Murfreesboro, Tennessee; and other places throughout the South

THE TIME:

John Cabell Breckinridge's lifespan, 1821–1875

I. CABELL AND JACOB

II. THE BATTLE

IV. EXILE AND FREEDMAN

" . . . we are united by an illusion,
by a tacit claim that there has been
no past. But there is that other life
we call our own, the life by whose light
or whose darkness, more likely darkness,
participation in the past is not a duty.
It is necessity."

> Richard Howard
> "A Phenomenon of Nature"
> *Two-Part Inventions*

" . . . one may begin rather than end with
the proposition that a nation's identity
is derived from the ways in which history
has . . . counterpointed certain opposite
potentialities; the ways in which it
lifts this counterpoint to a unique style
of civilization or lets it disintegrate
into mere contradiction."

> Erik Erikson
> *Childhood and Society*

" . . . from ancient grudge break to new mutiny,
where civil blood makes civil hands unclean."

> Shakespeare
> *Romeo and Juliet*

" . . . melody is born out of rhythm's needs."

> Robert Erickson
> *The Structure of Music*

CABELL AND JACOB
I

Cabell
MY MOTHER, THE WOMEN

Father and Mother had chills
and fever, but Father died,
calling her name like a prayer.
Finding the estate bankrupt,
Mother uttered no speech
for a month, except to weep.
Grandmother took us. I was
three, Laetitia a baby,
fretful even then,
her body stiff with screaming.
Mother opposes slavery —
feels we're a conquered nation
in an ocean of black, says
she begs even for shoes
for our feet: She weeps or shouts,
reads or sleeps. She mourns.

Easter, a woman at twelve,
cries in the kitchen, making
blueberry jam. She holds
a handful, blue, in her palm.
Look how blue they are,
she says, soft inside, and only
this morning, round and wild on
their shaggy bushes; she crushes
them by cupfuls in a pan.
Mister Will takes Easter
to his cabin — he used to
take Julene — to mend
his torn clothes. Maybe
you'll be free one day,
Easter, I say. Mother
thinks slavery's a sin.

I'll be free in heaven,
she says, wiping her nose
on her arm, and heaven's a long

way to climb. Mother's
father was a college president,
his father before him signed
the Declaration. Look
at me! she says. A prisoner!
Grandmother questions every
penny she spends, says
she and Father let money
make them its fools. Mother
dreams of slaves rising up,
taking back everything
they have built. She smells
the great house burning,

and I, at the edge of her bed,
singing the songs that Manda
patiently taught me to soothe her.

PORTRAITS OF THE FATHERS:
CABELL'S DALE

Father, I begged you to speak from the river,
and, again, you did not answer. Sparrows
skittered in circular baths of dust,
language, vague as your voice which I cannot
recall. I have seen eagles fall

from the sky into fields of corn, too full
of their previous hunt to lift the rabbit,
warm, back neatly broken by sharp
heels. The women in your Father's house
present their weapons: Grandmother's black

cap of mourning jerking animal-like,
Mother quoting your journals to her
response of quotes from Grandfather's books.
Laetitia sits alone in the kitchen
apart from the house: She will not

be cheered. No matter how I clown
for her, only Jacob can make
her laugh, dancing barefoot on the red
anthill, white shirt flying. In decency,

slave boys should wear field pants sooner;
I know you would agree. Last night,
alone in the great room, I spoke again
to the portraits, yours and Grandfather's: neither
answered. Your eyes stared straight ahead;

if anything moved, it was Grandfather's lips.

Cabell
LAETITIA, LITTLE SISTER

Laetitia has gone in the mud again.
Mister Will, the overseer, carries her
under the arms in front of him,
a small and naked offering, smeared

with wet mud. Suspended there
before him, her dark hair gleams
like our pond at night streaked
by the moon. She is silent till Mother

appears, then she begins to scream.
When our ewes were lambing, Laetitia
refused to sleep in the big house,
sat up all night in the barn, waiting.

Jacob sat with her, then held the lantern
high above as they searched the field,
stepping across wild peas and clover,
looking for newborns to bring inside.

Half the flock thinks she's their mother,
having seen her first by lantern light.
She has no fear; her empty bed
is cold before the family wakes.

Jacob listens for ravens to find her:
high in the ash, they mark her passage.
He goes to her, brings her to breakfast.
When Mother appears, Laetitia, muddy,

opens her mouth, screams, and mud
runs down her chin and blood runs down
her side from Mister Will's hand where she
has bitten him. Tish, Tish,

my beauty, why do you do it? Mother's
scream follows closely. Recoiling,

she calls Manda, refuses to touch her.
When Manda comes, crying, Lord,

Lord, Laetitia wraps dark
arms around Manda's neck. What
a sight they are! That muddy body
against Manda's white apron,

and Manda croons, Child, child, patting
the heaving back, her large hand
making sticky mud sounds
in the strange silence.

Cabell
THE REASONS I CRY

I cry when I think of the women's eyes, and I cry
when the hogs are butchered, hung upside down,
their lives dripping red through their own mouths,
and I cry after summer storms, the leaves, their green
increased through rain's intense eye, and I cry
to hear how silently the dead porcupine
by the side of the road tucks away
his quills, and I cry in spite of Mother's frown,
and I cry to see the boys, after catching
a pregnant cat, dancing on her back, and I cry
for Easter, grown into a woman now and lost,
and I cry for baby birds, their beaks swaying
open on slender necks no bigger than
my finger, and I cry when I hear the slaves
sing, Carry me home, Lord, please carry me home,
and I cry when I think of Grandfather, dead
at forty-six, and Father, dead at thirty-five,
and I cry because the world is so big,
and I don't know if I'm big enough
to do what needs to be done
to end this crying. . . .

Jacob
HOW I LEARN: FIVE VERSES
FOR BANJO AND BONES (i)

Though she knows better,
Young Mistress Laetitia gives me
words for keeps: *bad, beg, big, boy, buy,*
shows me how to please and thank-you,
bow from the waist, eyes closed, teaches me
how white folks talk, bodies pulled back
like the coach mare, soft talk, smaller even
than our God songs whispered out after midnight
in the woods, sung into a cooking pot to catch
the stray word, songs whispered loud
as we dare, tricking the Patterrollers into
our not being there at all, unless they bring
along their dogs—those growls, those teeth
and claws. Then, even our singing
cannot lift us high enough.

Jacob

HOW I LEARN: FIVE VERSES
FOR BANJO AND BONES (ii)

Young Mistress Laetitia gets ideas,
and some of them are bad. She calls the lambs
her angels, dreams that red wolves
eat them, half-born, as they cry out
like babies: *care, cream, circle, cord, cure.*
That night the ewes are lambing, she has me
hold the lantern high, while she
bends over, helps them come outside.
Wind blows those flames wicked,
throws them around the field.
She laughs at me, says my eyes
are showing white. I say, by moonlight,
her dark hair's what wolves like best,
and then she laughs and laughs.
When she stands to hold the new lamb,
she whispers, Angel, angel, her face splashed
red with birth blood. Just after sunset,
I hear something close to my head,
duck down as wings touch my ear,
then laugh to see it's only a swallow
hunting late supper in lantern light.

Jacob

HOW I LEARN: FIVE VERSES
FOR BANJO AND BONES (iii)

Late one day, I doze off by the spring,
wake up after dark. Afraid to move,
I back up close to an old white oak,
get myself smaller. All night, dark
things try to enter me. Witches ride by
on the sleeping souls, whip them while they
cry out like babies, beg to rest,
but witches don't listen — they got holes
where hearts should be. Somehow I live
through it, next day, tell Grampa Sam,
and he says I've been chosen,
chosen for telling stories, says this gift
means all God's world is my best friend,
means not a house won't open
its door to me, not a man or woman
whose story I can't know, just look
in the eyes, and if the eyes shut,
the heart will tell it out
through the face: *dare, dread, dig,*
door, duty. This gift, he says,
was his, now passing over to me.
After he says that, I sleep
the day away. Somewhere in my head,
I hear his dark voice singing.

Jacob
THIS FIRST STORY, I, JACOB, TELL

one hot day, old woman made of wind swells up, opens
her windy mouth, dark as the devil's closet, wide
as the devil's grin, wails out long and sad enough
to make a scarecrow cry, and a small blue swallow
flies out from her mouth, a swallow beautiful and blue
as water to the burning hour: he spreads out his wing,
covers the flaming sun's face, holds within his beak
golden bolts of lightning, sends them sailing, stitching
threads of fire across miles of blue cloth: kiri, kiri,
kiri, sings the small blue swallow, and the sky darkens
with clouds that shout out promise after promise, and
the man most tired and the woman most weary, shoulders
bent over with work, lift their eyes from the ground up
to the promising sky, as if their loads are lighter
than the cool drops of rain falling on their dusty faces

Cabell
JACOB'S TOOTH

May, the sweetness of moist
grass, the universe drawing
its first deep breath

of creation, the sun singing
its early morning song

in a sky clear
of a single covering cloud.

Our boy, Jacob, leans grinning
against the front gate,
proud, having lost

before us his first baby tooth.
Laetitia washes it,
winds it in her white ribbon.

We hear the hum of all
that is newly hatched,

the buzz of what feeds
on that tender delivery,

as we pull the wrapped tooth
in the wagon to the slave plot.

White apple blossoms blow off
the trees, float past
on the river, deceptive islands,

scented and moving, water
appearing to freeze beneath them.

I read the Bible passage
about this life
and the next, and with full

ceremony, we bury the tooth, crown
to the west, slave-style, singing
Swing low sweet chariot,
comin' for to carry me home.

When Jacob begins to cry,
both of us join in,
Laetitia unable to stop,

until we run to the hill
by the river, roll down,
roll out of control

over hummocks and valleys, crushing
new blades of grass
under our turning

bodies, out of control, dazed
on movement, dizzy on speed,
arrive at the bottom

unable to stand. We lie on our backs,
silently stare at the blue
sky we can find no beginning

or end for. Feeling light
as summer air, our bodies defined
by the outline of flattened grass

around them, we cannot remain,
float away on the unexplored
rivers of three separate lives.

Cabell
MY GRANDMOTHER BLACK CAP

Before walking Grandmother
on her rounds, if Annie,
her body servant, is busy,
she has me button the back
of her dress. When Grandfather
died, she buried her sight
with him. She'll be laid
beside him in his coffin
when her time comes.
In Grandfather's room of law,
slave-built, she tells
stories to me. Men rode
from three states to sit
at his feet. Spring bloom,
and the mares come around—
her hand on the stallion's
drenched shoulder, he stills.
She must touch the new calves
and new lambs, knows every bird
by its song, calls me Cabell
like my father. She never removes
her black cap of mourning.
Last night after dinner,
she heard a new bird, insisted
I lead her to it down
the tangle of brush at the river.
We never got close enough—
a wren, perhaps, but a log
gave way, tumbled us down
to the river's edge, soaking
my pant legs, the hem
of her dress. How Annie
scolded us! I dream
Grandfather's grave opens,
but I will not release
her, grasp her hand
until she glides out

of her human flesh —
bone so white —
those arms a brittle yoke
around my neck. I wake,
pleading. She calls my poor
mother Her Majesty.
Mother calls her
The Dark Queen.

Cabell

MOVING FROM VIRGINIA TO KENTUCKY—GRANDMOTHER SHOWS ME A LETTER SENT TO GRANDFATHER FROM COLONEL THOMPSON WHO TOOK OUR SLAVES TO KENTUCKY AND THEN HIRED THEM OUT: JUNE 1792

Mister John Breckinridge, Virginia:
It is done, and not an hour too soon.
Approaching the River Monongahela, Red Stone
on its banks appeared a Second Eden—
our Whiskey, its blonde Mercy, had just
run dry. To tell the Truth, it got us there.
You know how they wailed when we left; it never ceased.
Six weeks, this trip, and four through mud
up to our knees, or snow and ice that froze
our hands and feet. I don't know what was worse,
flesh frozen or thawed with this result—
the soles of our feet peeled off in our hands
like bacon. I'm sorry to report we lost the wagon
in a slide that nearly claimed us all,
but Sam refused to let the horses go,
saved them both, the bay a little lame.
If I could name them, I'd call our Mountains Misery.
The Floods our first assault, every River
overflowed its banks to roughly claim
the neighboring house and field—trees sprouting
families, one a flock of hens and two cats.
(Is this the Fruit you speak of in Kentucky?)
We crossed a field, burned black except
for three spears, each waving a skull
like a white flag. Indians, we guessed,
Shawnee. We could not explain
the assemblage of small birds, blue and red,
circling the charred remains of the field, singing.
We had to chain the slaves from that day on.
Then the Mountains—and the rain, a River

pouring continuous night and day. Our canvas
tents bowed and poured on us like pitchers.
You know how slaves detest the high ground.
They dropped with every Thunder clap, thought
Lightning a lash splitting the Sky to face
them with their God—and this a furious fellow.
If it were not for Sam, his influence,
I would have lost them all at the final Summit.
Two men, I guess they were, freedmen,
though it was hard to tell, strung upside
down from the branch of a Poplar tree,
the feet gone, the heads too, and this
mutilation the last straw for the slaves, who fell
on the ground and would not move, prepared to die.
It was then I brought out our good friend, Whiskey,
gave them a shot every hour they weren't asleep,
and this way—some of them sick, some of them singing—
I brought them over the Mountains into Jordan.
They rested at Colonel Meredith's before we let
them out for hire. What a cry they put up!
to leave, a second time, their friends and relations.
Although we got less for the two old ones,
Sam and John brought Six Pounds, the childless
women, Three, women with children, Fifty
Shillings, and two boys at Eighteen apiece.
The Twenty Pounds of my advance covered
the journey's supplies. The trip itself demands
forgetting. I trust this letter finds you well.
Remaining yours, Sincerely, Colonel Thompson

Cabell

WHAT GRANDMOTHER BLACK CAP TOLD ME: TAKING THE FAMILY WEST TO KENTUCKY, MARCH 1793

               All I remember
is mud and loss
and rutted roads and loss, more loss,

and four small children, muddy, clinging
to me, a tree on a shifting
plain (falling,

falling away from friends,
away from all I knew and loved).

John said I buried my smile
back in Virginia. I feared I'd dig
five graves — and then my own.

               To willingly enter
savagery (at the time I couldn't forgive
him). Laetitia was seven,

your father, almost five, Mary
was four and little Robert
barely toddling.

               Your grandfather's books —
one-hundred-fifty of them, filled
one wagon. Thirteen volumes of *Debates*
In Parliament. (Could we debate the mud?)

And Shakespeare — ten volumes
of history and passion — eloquence against
incessant rain that soaked and swelled them!

               A book for a muddy mile —
Paradise lost and not regained,
one-hundred-fifty miles of unremitting torture,

and, for solace, Inns disgusting
in their filth and poor food. The quarters

for the women cold, wood too wet to burn,
help backward and sullen.

                                 (In one, not even warmed water
                                 or towels to wash and dry us!)

Our children's health ran out
through their dripping noses — or the other way.

I watched their eyes grow large, glaze over.
Their tiny bodies shriveled before my eyes.

                     · · ·

And then the river, swollen
with spring thaw, running fast
as a fox, the dogs close behind,

our boat of oaken planks
frail as a leaf upon it.

The smoke we breathed, the drafty
cabin, our fear

                                 for the children, their lives
                                 carried off in the river's arms.

Then one night in alien land, trees
haloed in crimson light, we heard
our names called out clearly
from the shore:

Polly! A woman's voice. Then,
John! I need your help, please,
they have me. Please help!

On the far bank, a woman,
blonde, holding a child,

a fair child, crying. Behind her,
shadows, or were they trees? No,
they moved. Indians!

(John said they listened
to us talk, learned
our names upstream
by water's magnification.)

Knowing it a lure tempting us
like fish to the bank to catch,

then kill us all,
John shouted, Hold fast!
Steer straight ahead!

Our house servants set up
an awful wail, the children too,

                    joining that fair child on shore,
                    and then our names called out

                    again,
                         again. . . .

All these years, echoing
through my dreams, that blonde woman
we could not save,

her dress of pale blue torn
at the waist. She calls

and calls me still,

shadows moving in

upon her. . . .

Cabell
MOTHER'S BOOKS

Mother's reading her books again.

Sitting outside, flies fanned away
by Easter, she strokes my hair,
hardly knows I'm beside her.

This morning, she argued with Grandmother
about my schooling, feels Uncle Robert
should give me a proper education
away from home.

She weeps for what she cannot give.
She reads.

Grandmother forbids certain books,
like Richardson's *Clarissa* novel,
says it's immoral to feel so much

at another's expense. That poor
unfortunate has enough to carry
without your sorrow, she says.

Grandmother approves of moral books,
ones that help you bear your burdens

in silence. Mother reads Richardson
alone, hidden from Grandmother's glares.

Sometimes Jacob and I sit beside her.
I like it when she reads to us;

then I know she's here.

She teaches us how to spell the words.
Grandmother would be furious
if she knew. Mother thinks Jacob's

adorable—and so quick. She dresses
him up, talks to him about freedom;

then both of them look sad.

Grandmother says such talk only
makes the slaves restless, expecting
what they can never have.

Often Mother looks at me
as if I'm a stranger, begins to sob.
Poor boy, she says, You've inherited

nothing but debts from your father.
No land. No money. Just the little
grudgingly given by relations.

She can't forgive Uncle Robert who
told her Father's estate was embarrassed.

Embarrassed!
She says it as if my uncle chose it so.

Not even enough to live on
like a family, she says.

Squatters in your grandmother's house!

You must do it alone—no land, no money,
little else than a name,
and a name can't buy food for your table.

When she reads Richardson's book,
how Clarissa ran away from her parents,

Mother's breathing quiets,
some of her goes there.

It frightens me. She doesn't return
when I call. Her shape on the couch dims,

grows dimmer. One day she'll fade;
I'll see the rose design of the couch

through her. She'll be gone, except
for the distant sound of weeping.
The roses.

Cabell

WITH LAETITIA AT THE
INDIAN MOUNDS, CABELL'S DALE

Digging for arrowheads, then deeper
to a skull, we are frightened
by the eyes looking through us to our bones,

but when Laetitia laughs, it lends us
its magic. To my trembling lips, she holds
her cut finger, calls me twice-brother in blood,

and as she dances upon the raised earth,
she moves slowly, as if in a trance, toward the trees.
A large buck, mossy antlers branching up

to nearly double his height, stands and watches,
allows her almost to touch him before whirling
and fading, like smoke, into the woods.

We pick wild iris, purple, and prairie
rose, each pink fist relaxing
before the petals bruise and fall.

We pray the Indian way. Soft-shelled turtles
come to us from the creek, and we build a fire,
fry them for our hunger. Red-spotted skink

touch our faces cooly with their
flat fingers. We laugh, then still, twice
blessed, by one another and the world.

Jacob

HOW I LEARN: FIVE VERSES
FOR BANJO AND BONES (iv)

I bend down low in the stable, spend
all day with the fillies, thoroughbreds
brought over from England in boats.
Two bay, one chestnut, and two
white, all white, eyes
so black they shine backwards.
Running, they leave the wind behind,
can jump any fence on the Dale: *fast,*
faster, fastest. Freedom. Flight.
I see, in the sunlight sneaking between the beams,
dust carrying the smell of hay into my nose.
All day I hear their hard feet first rise up,
then stamp down, hear them chew their
grain from pails, see the red flower, damp
with dew, twice bloom inside their noses, the sun
catch, shine out from their brushed shoulders.
I feel their warm skin shiver.
When the Mistress finds me, she beats
me good, pulls both my ears, but it
is worth it—their eyes, that shine,
their long long legs.

CIVIL BLOOD

Jacob
MOVING TO THE BIG HOUSE

How I wanted, Young Master,
the pine-floor mattress
by your big oak bed.
sun may set   but never dies
Eight little niggers, eight empty bellies,
all of us doing our tricks, trying
to be your playboy.
moon is round   but cannot roll
My mother coaches me instead of sleep,
knowing what the Mistress likes.
Then she scrapes and scrubs me good!
spirit of white oak   give me strength
Cartwheels, one-foot hopping,
backwards sommersets, I can stand twice
the time of holding my breath
hands of the world   support me
on my head, shirt of homespun
dropping down around my face,
and the Mistress, her mad look,
eyes of the world   look kindly on me
never once lowers her eyes,
laughs when old Master Rooster
pecks at my trying fingers.
ears of the world   hear my prayer
Most likely, my crazy, high-
jumping dance won her, she
laughs so she can hardly
hare gets hunted   but he can run
talk, pointing, she says, You're
the one, pointing, You, Jacob,
and to my mother, Scrape
bee gets the honey   fly gets the rest
off that dirt and wash him
well now, won't you Manda.
Later, a suit of tow linen
inch worm gets there   just gets there slower
comes from the Big House.

Because of my blood, I have more
at stake than the rest.
river of indigo   river of blood
To leave the dirt floors
of our shack, the three-
to-a-bed, the Patterrollers,
black night finds   a voice for screaming
to eat the meats from the Big House,
wear shoes that fit, escape
the fields they feed us to.
cur dog could sing   if he had a song
I swear, I have never jumped higher!

Jacob
WHAT GRAMPA SAM TOLD ME:
THE OLD DAYS IN VIRGINIA

in the beginning, this new land. so much land a young
buck slave can walk—can even run—two whole days, not
lay eyes on half of it,

land throwing up wild grass to the sky like a prayer,
praise the lord! high grass, good grass, animals grow
slick and fat for the table.

when we are little, we trick deer to our bows and
arrows with salt licks, catch partridge and quail,

snare them up with spring branch and loop—the possum
and the coon, they nearly walk up and introduce
themselves to you!

we do task work, master john trusts us, leaves us alone
if we work, and, young and strong as midnight, I always
work—sun to sun, can to can't,

clearing the land, knocking down shrub and tree and thick
thick grass to plant a crop.

once I hear the big oak speak to me as he falls, I
just act deaf—can't do nothing about it—but my ears
remember.

our labor brings that land around, dirt so rich and black
it nearly takes the seed out from our hands, does the
planting its own self. I was a wonder with a hoe!

. . .

it takes a spell, but they make us work that land to death—
if a slave's sick you can bleed him, feed him bacon and corn
bread, pick herbs from the woods—blue moss, quinine,
calomel—

you can boil up a potion—snakeroot, larkspur, redroot—
and he can down it with persimmon wine, but ain't nothing
you can give a dying field when they're bound on working
it to death.

how we hate to see something die we've worked so much
labor on!

corn takes more than her share, rustling so mighty fine
proud, waving her long yellow hair out above
that green dress, tight as skin is,

and the same year, they have us put in wheat or rye,
fields worked harder even than we are, never given a
rest, never planted in sweet clover, never given shade

from that devil sun, and then, tobacco to polish off the
job, those brown leaves drinking up the little life
that's left—

land dead and gone for even hay or pasture, all grown
up in scrub cedar, chinquapin bush, sedge grass, blue

at the tops, a shelter for rabbits and field mice,
not fit for grazing, for feeding anything at all.

• • •

land that grew our crops year after year—longer than
we can remember—is still there, but gone, used up,

finished, and this dead land still holds our graves,
one body, then another, broken to that blooming.

on week nights, our old preacher says god's wrath comes
down from heaven, god's punishment grows up from the dust,

and sorrow shall they eat three meals a day,

and we that are singing, that are praying and weeping,
know—lord deliver us—their sorrow is our sorrow. . . .

CABELL AND JACOB

Jacob

HOW I LEARN: FIVE VERSES
FOR BANJO AND BONES (v)

All through plow, hay, harvest, and wind,
I carry water to the dusty hoe slave,
the plow slave, the one planting corn,
the one planting hemp, the one too worn-out
to work. I carry water to Jenny,
passed out in the shade of the chestnut tree,
three months after little Darrel comes,
Jenny, who's born fourteen head
of children, five of them alive:
law, least, lied, low, luck. Bleeding
still, she cannot drink. I rip off, careful,
the sleeve of my coarse shirt, dip it
in my water pail, wipe out dirt and sweat
from her closed eyes. She moans, asks for Ben,
forgetting he got auctioned off last month
by Master Webb next door. Ben, her
'broad husband, showed too much liking
for Jenny, won't stay 'broad where
he's supposed to be. By now, he's
probably down river, but I don't
say down river to her, don't say
down river to no-
body.

CIVIL BLOOD

Cabell

WITH LAETITIA AT THE INDIAN MOUNDS, CABELL'S DALE: A MASSACRE OF PASSENGER PIGEONS

All night we hear them flying, a thunder of wings.
Morning, branches broken, our clearing is plastered
with droppings, carpeted with hundreds of birds.

A massacre of Passenger Pigeons, killed trying
to rest the night, crushed by their own weight,
birds landing—layer after layer—on dying birds.
I am terrified. Laetitia's eyes

get round and dark as theirs. She falls
to her knees among them, smooths their feathers, straightens
their twisted necks, arranges them in patterns.

We carry them back to the house—it takes us hours—
Manda warns us, says the women won't like it.
We carry them back to the house, armfuls of birds

dropping beside the path like feathered flowers,
bluer by far than the sky they've left behind.
When Sam drives Mother and Grandmother home in the carriage,

pigeons are piled so high on the portico
they cover the top of the door. Mother blames
Manda, shouts at her, cries and cries,

hitting her on the back with her hand,
Manda and Sam running, long after the sun
has set, back to the woods with dead birds.

Jacob
THIS SECOND STORY, I, JACOB, TELL

the blue swallow flies to the little water boy,
lands on his shoulder, tells him to pull out one
of his blue feathers, hold it over the pond until
the pond speaks, and this the little water boy does:
kiri, kiri, kiri, the swallow cries in pain, but he
gives up one of his feathers: the boy holds it over
the water, and his eyes can't hardly believe themselves:
rising up slowly from the no-bottom black of the pond,
a coffin made of reeds whose green hands hold a woman's
worn-out body, a body that looks just like jenny,
whose heart ran out between her legs following
after the life of her fourteenth child: and the boy
touches jenny with the blue feather, and she sits up,
singing, and the blood obeys, comes back to its home,
her heart, and she feels new again, as before the burden
of children entered into the belly of her child body

Jacob
WHAT GRAMPA SAM TOLD ME:
YOUR GRAMMA,
SHE CAME OFF THE BOAT

black and big as this here door top,
mean as any trapped thing, bad

    as something big as that can be—

       except to me, the only one she softens for.

celia they call her, such a fly-butter name for that
hurricane woman, but she is celia to me, my 'broad wife.

master john writes me a pass both wednesday and saturday
nights—

    I never see her in daylight except at christmas
    when I'm there with her a week,

and she can dance
          so wild it turns me that way too!

traders trick her on that boat with gold bracelets,
get her down—it takes three of them to chain her—

and she fights them so they beat her near to death,

    and has the back to prove it.

she wears those bracelets all right, but they ain't any
gold, and she never
        gets religion,
             and she never once forgives.

      . . .

at first celia takes off her dress in the field when it
is hot, says she works better without it, but they are

telling her,

       put it on,

           put it on now, celia.

master webb, he lays an eye on her, but too scared
about coming close enough to touch.

I see her dance just once, and that is that,
I have to have her,
          and she agrees.

                 master webb thinks
                 and thinks on it,

till finally he says yes because he wants them little
niggers, and he's too scared to get them for himself.

          • • •

we jump over the broom,

          she drops four in four years,

and two of them stillborn, and one is funny in its head.
only little manda makes it through okay.

but master webb comes on bad times, takes to cursing celia,
tells her he's gonna' put her in his pocket, and she says
he don't dare,
        so he comes at her with his big bullsnake,

and she stands there,

hoe raised, saying,

come on master!
come on close now!

I beg master john to buy her, but he says she's too mean,
and no matter how I beg, all he says is no, and it
isn't but a week before those soul drivers sneak right out

in the field,
get her from behind, and master webb
sells her down river, laughs when they pay him,

says, I put you in my pocket now, celia, just like I
promised.

this slave so low, can't hardly lift his head,

so master john buys up manda, and she's all that's
left alive of celia.

and each and every day, I lift myself up,
speak so to the sky, say, morning wife,

you preparing to fight your way through another day?

Cabell

AT ELEVEN, I WRITE TO LAETITIA
FROM KENTUCKY ACADEMY

My Darling Sister, I miss you
most remembering the jokes
we played—pink ribbon
around the neck of the Blacksnake
I gave you for your birthday;
the possum skull you put
under my covers—feeling
for warmth, my poor feet
received a toothy surprise!
Shooting white-tail deer
with Uncle Robert, I often
aim high, can't bear the
blood that's run from their mouths
when we reach them.
Last week I shot
a mallard, my first, held it
in my hands, its limp
neck, head swinging
heavy. Red, like spilled
ink, slowly stained its
iridescent green.
Don't ask me why, I wept,
demeaning myself with Uncle
Robert, who saved my pride
by saying nothing. Laetitia,
don't darken your shiny
days with loneliness.
I'll soon be home again.
Next summer will be
as before. There's more joy
for me in school than I
knew the world allowed.
Since a man betrays
himself by his speech,
I memorize a word
a day, test myself

at each week's end.
My first debate was splendid!
Taking the anti-slavery
position, I proved beyond a
doubt that slavery's not
a choice morality allows.
It must be slowly abolished.
Uncle Robert was proud
when he learned of my
success. Having freed
five of his own slaves
already, he strongly favors
colonization in Africa,
the owners fairly paid.
Is Jacob taking care
of you? I miss him, wonder
if he goes to Africa
how he'll pack all
his shoes, and still have
room for anything else!
(Mother spoils him so.)
I'm reading Demosthenes,
commit Pericles
to memory. My friend,
William Birney, and I
read *The Last of the
Mohicans*. Now we're Indians,
riding the plains on milk-
white ponies. (If you
were here, you'd play the Maiden
we capture, though with your temper
you'd be a challenge
for the fiercest brave!) Try
to make some new friends,
and please be better to Mama
as she can't help

it. I love you more
than anyone alive.
Your only brother, Cabell

Cabell

LAETITIA WRITES BACK TO ME

I hate to hear how happy you are,
as if we were the sadness you left behind!

and don't tell me not to be lonely—
even our spotted
hound has curled up in the corner and died—
and don't tell me it will ever
be the same—
all that summer does is end—
and don't joke that Jacob's going
to Africa—
he does nothing but sulk, missing you—
and don't tell me to make
some new friends—
I'll talk with lizards and white moths—
and don't tell me to get along
with mama—
every day is deaf with her thunder—
and don't tell me that you love
your horrible school—
it's a cartful of words and more words—

that pony of william birney's can gallop
into a haystack for all I care

and pericles can perish too—
I go to our Indian mounds, their

voices call out to me—
they want me to ride away with them—

they want to race me there—maybe
I'll come to you that way—

THANKSGIVING: THE STOLEN CIGAR

During the grown-ups' party,
when, high on the breeze
of laughter, the voices rise
as if everyone has suddenly
flung away his hearing, I

creep down the carpeted hall
to the closet, steal a cigar
from Major Maguffin's pocket.

Crunching across downed
leaves—browns and yellows—
I wrap my own coat, thin
against the wind, around me,

meet Jacob at the Meat House.
Too windy to get it lit
outside, we sit in sawdust,

smoke it down, rolling it
between thumb and third finger,
putting it under our wrinkled noses,

smelling it like the Major does,
laughing till we are blinded
by our own tears. The tallow candle

falters in the wind
blowing through the cracks
between boards, our shadows,

ominous, dancing drunkenly
with the hanging slabs of meat.
A moth, jailed in the fry
of melted wax, flares up,

grim warning. We're coughing now,
and, half in laughter, half in fear,
we snuff the cigar against the ice,
feeling just a little sick.

Sitting there with Jacob—dizzy,
arms wrapped around our legs,
chins upon our knees—I think
I'll never love anyone more.

The way he looks at me, brown eyes
swimming with what he cannot say,
I know he feels the same.

No matter what we do, that smell
of cigar will not shoo away.

It has sunk into sawdust,
the swaying red of hams, even into
blocks of ice, their solid squares.

All of it stares back at us,
the blank stare of evidence
indelibly stamped and sealed.

Wind blows all that night,
my dreams flung back and forth
like our empty children's swing.

When Grandmother peers into my
eyes the next day, her own eyes,
their blacks filmed over

with blindness, peers into
my eyes as if she's seen it all,
and asks me if I was smoking,

I dare not lose her love,
say Jacob smokes. She leans
closer, and I swear that it is true.

Soon, I hear him crying, know
she's switching his legs.

I run to the fields, climb
the oak, swing up on its lowest
limb, sit all day there

above the fields, picked clean
under fall's clustering sparrows,
the hazy sun. Returning home,

my plundered branch, stripped bare
of leaves, slices off the golden
heads of grass bordering the path,
and I'm angry, angry at Jacob.

By the time I sit down for supper,
see his face in the hall, eyes
swollen with tears, the whole thing —

by now gone up in smoke —
seems his idea.

He tries a little smile
on me, but I'll have none
of it, scowl hard at him

over the candle's pale flicker,
a look I hope he knows
means he must never

do such a thing again.
Never again.

CIVIL BLOOD

Jacob
THIS THIRD STORY, I, JACOB, TELL

the grapes hang black on the vine when the little
water boy sits on the bank of the rushing river,
the corn stands gold on the stalk when the little
water boy asks, o great and moving water, please
carry me away, but the river's too busy finding
his way to the sea, can't stop to give any water
boy a ride, so the boy looks up to the sky, asks
the wind, o great and powerful wind, please carry
me away, but the wind has no heart in her, till
the small blue swallow flies down to sit upon
his shoulder: kiri, kiri, kiri, he cries, tells
the boy to put on the little blue coat he carries
in his beak, and the water boy laughs, the blue
coat's so small he can't even get one finger in
the tiny sleeve, but he tries, and then the little
coat, this water-blue coat, this sky-blue coat
grows big enough to put it on: kiri, kiri, kiri,
cries the small blue swallow, follow me, and he
spreads his feather wings just to show him what
to do, and the boy spreads out his arms: the wind
finds her heart behind a cloud, reaches down
under the arms of the little water boy, lifts
him to the sky where the boy dips and glides,
light as a small blue feather: he goes to visit
all those he loves and longs to see, finds his
gramma who's gone far away far, and she holds him
on her lap, puts her strong arms around him, sings
him a mighty song, a song he's never heard
before from africa across the sea, and the song
she sings begins like this: kiri, kiri, kiri

Cabell
LAETITIA'S ESCAPE

At fifteen, Laetitia's grown tall,
dark hair curling out wild
from a careless center part.

Boys, awkwardly shy, come to her
in groups, but she's disdainful.

Her eyes growing darker,
more perfect,

she criticizes, to their faces,
how they dress or talk.

She walks alone
or with me, home from college
on vacation, begs me again to stay.

She walks faster, shadow's
child; I can't keep
up with her. Cabell!

she cries out to me one night,
I wanted us never to change!

Leaving early in the morning,
she often misses supper,
Mother fuming, pacing about as usual.

Laetitia, womb-child Mother carried
when Father died, as if forced
to trade in one for the other.

Poor child, poor Mother, drying
bone-white in the desert
of our borrowed home.

Jacob patiently searches for her,
mixing her name with the slave
songs he's always singing,

but Laetitia escapes her sorrowful
name sung out again and again.

One day she tells me about the time—
she must have been five or six—
when she wouldn't stop crying,

and Mother held her up,
raised high above her head,
held her over the river,

threatened to throw her in.
At first I can't believe it,
but Laetitia convinces me it's true,

smiles at my shock.
In her face, I see what a smile

disguises, how a branch
is broken by the weakest wind.

She walks quickly, as if speed
could help her escape
whatever chases her.

The end of summer, willows turning
yellow with the lack of rain,
daylight raw as a wound,

I come upon her by the river,
surrounded by grazing mares,
their leggy batch of bay foals.

She's laid out a picnic for two
on a white spread,

her hair a dark storm above it.

The air hangs August-heavy with heat.
She's laughing with someone

I can't see, her cheeks flushed
pink. I'm pleased to know

she's with a friend.
It's some time before I see
that she's alone.

Cabell

JOURNAL ENTRIES: PREPARING
FOR PUBLIC OFFICE

APRIL 20, 1839: PRINCETON, NEW JERSEY

Uncle Robert has rescued his penniless nephew again,
taken me into his home while I study at Princeton for
the law exam. He and I argue politics until my aunt
holds her ears. My sympathy lies with Jackson's
Democrats, the hard-working man, unburdened by slaves
or inherited property, building our country's tomorrow
from the ground up. Uncle Robert, a Whig like the
rest of the family, fears I caught this attitude
at Princeton where the air is full of such talk.

Uncle Robert has done a great deal for me. Having so little
to give in return, sometimes I feel reduced to the scraping
smile of gratitude. Thank you is such a small offering.

I find that exercise and daily regularity, a regimen favoring
both of these, the key to fitness of mind and body. I keep
my schedule realistic, unlike my classmate at Centre College
who studied sixteen hours a day, but for want of daily
exercise sat in a stupor, half-awake and only half-asleep.

In preparation for the task at hand, I read the law
seven hours a day, then three hours more of literature
and history, until my mind is stuffed with all that it
can reasonably hold. I study my list of self-improvements
daily. There's still much work to be done! I keep the list
in my pocket so I can constantly impress these qualities
of character on my memory:

1. When you speak to a person, look him in the eye.
   (I often drop my eyes from shyness, like a
   chicken thief caught with a fistful of feathers!)

2. Good company and good conversation are the very
   bone and muscle of virtue. (This one is easy
   for me—too easy I fear.)

3. Avoid temptation—you may not be able to resist
   it. (If I'd do less of the second one, the
   third would be easier!)

It's difficult for me to maintain a regular study schedule.
When friends tempt me to pleasure, I find it impossible
to resist. Then I study much too hard trying to regain the
time I've lost, only to fall ill from exhaustion.

But I love to be with people, love good conversation!
Yesterday, I read they've added sleeping cars to trains.
Sleeping cars! People stacked up like firewood, but asleep,
speeding across the earth, falling asleep in one state and
opening their weary morning eyes in another!

One day I'll travel by train. Perhaps I'll even own one.
But first I must go west and make my fortune so I can
return to Lexington in style. In my own train. I'll have
the whole thing to myself so I won't be too crowded—
well, maybe one or two of my closest friends can join me—
but we will keep a rational schedule of work and leisure.

MAY 20, 1842: BURLINGTON, IOWA

Although I'm a graduate of law, I need enlightenment on how
a young lawyer can survive on payments of beets, potatoes,
and raw onions! This frontiersman, after a full year's hard
work, has accumulated a rented room, one straw mattress and
a broom—the broom is robust, the mattress sorely lacking.

All winter I curled, shivering, under my buffalo robe, snow
sifting in through the ill-fitted boards known as walls.

This morning, the woman of the house is baking bread. Its
welcome aroma rises up between the floorboards. Outside,

her children, clustered under my window, pick bouquets of purple violets for their mother; their tiny fists clutch the stems so tightly, you'd think the blossoms wanted to escape.

My heart floods—first with love for everything alive, then loneliness—back and forth and back again.

I keep thinking about last fall's buffalo hunt, how perfectly the Fox Indians accommodate their lives to nature. Mornings were hazy, blue from miles of swaying grass, until the sun rose to light up hundreds of yellow flowers. The Indians must be God's favorite children. How can He ever forgive us for what we've done to them?

I have never felt so moved as when Chief Keokuk spoke that night. He stood on a mound of dirt, all eyes raised to him; his stature, his carriage, the words and gestures he chose were more elegant than anything I've ever experienced. At that moment, I knew I must carry on the tradition of my Father and my Father's Father and enter politics. Yet I couldn't understand a word he said!

OCTOBER 5, 1843: LEXINGTON, KENTUCKY

After returning in June for what I thought would be a short visit to replenish my spirits and health, I fell almost immediately in love. Her name is Mary Cyrene Burch. She loves me with a devotion I didn't know possible. She, too, has been raised by relatives, having lost her parents young. It comforts us both to bear that loss together. We are engaged to be married in December. I've already liquidated my practice in Burlington, totaled my assets—sixty-eight dollars! Mary's relatives have convinced me to return to Lexington, set up my practice here so that I may represent them. They have significant holdings in slaves and land,

not only in Kentucky, but in Mississippi and Louisiana too.
They fear the government means to interfere with their
property.

I've thought long and hard about this alliance, since I'd
hoped to escape the South's dark burden. Once married,
my fate is sealed with those owning slaves. But a man
who's inherited a name and no land must make a living.

No one disputes the fact that slavery is detestable—
an evil inherited from our fathers. But the South is built
upon that grim foundation; without its support, we fall.
Government interference with the property it's been
established to protect is tyranny. Perhaps it's
possible to find a just way for both free and slave.

How fine it is to be in love! I'm convinced that one woman
contains both day and night, sunset and sunrise, fair and
cloudy skies. I feel like a blind man given sight!

THREE STUDIES FOR THE PAINTING OF CABELL'S BRIDE, MARY CYRENE BURCH, IN THE YEAR 1843

I.

Hair pulled back, tight
at the neck, ears covered.
She's wealthy, family connections
in education, slaves, and land.
How to paint that? Make
the mouth firm, chin slightly
protruding, a strong face, yet
submissive. Used to being served.

II.

Dark hair, dark eyes,
straight line of a mouth,
lips pulled in, nearly hidden.
Spends time in bed—chills
and fever—undisclosed complaints.
The background should be muted,
and she, at seventeen, obedient,
playing the role prescribed.

III.

Eyes veiled, lace collar
held in place by an ivory brooch.
Her expression, though blurred,
is compassionate. She will call
her husband Precious, nearly
die bearing their first child.
Paint her just about to speak,
changing her mind.

Cabell
THE WEDDING

Flowers cover everything,
fiddlers play, pigs
sizzle and turn on the spit,
apples red in their mouths,
as our two hearts throb,
beat like drums in our wrists,
in our throats, in our dancing feet,
dancing away the days
and the nights, Manda's huge body
shaking and wailing and crying
whenever she comes upon me,
and Jacob, in one of his colorful
get-ups put together
on my behalf, complete with
red shoes and red shirt,
and oh how he dances, spinning,
then jumping, turning around
and around and around, white
flowers turning with him,
and I, made bold by good
bourbon, jump up and join him,
and then pull up Mary,
by now, laughing so hard
she abruptly sits down on
her feet, dress billowing
out like a cloud come down
to join this rollicking heaven,
and later, still giddy, she
presents Major Maguffin
to her witless husband
as Muffin, and Major Muffin
he is to this day, and we eat
till our clothes won't contain us,
dancing the fiddlers' arms
nearly off their bouncing
bodies, and when we get
to our room, alone, petals

of summer roses strewn
upon our bed, finally
alone, it is so
quiet, so incredibly
still, we can find
nothing to say to lead us
through this charged silence
into our life together.

CIVIL BLOOD

Cabell
RUNNING FOR STATE
REPRESENTATIVE: SUMMER 1849

I.

Some men feel alone in crowds,
but I feel most alive, most at home
surrounded by the disarray
of people gathered together.

Even my horse prances in anticipation
as I ride the length of Fayette County,
speak to any gathering that will listen.

Arriving two or three hours early,
I mix among them, chatting,

then stand above the crowd
on tree stumps, empty wagon beds,
the courthouse steps, to speak.

They turn toward me as I give thanks
to Jefferson for my ideals, to Jackson
for my politics, my faith in the common man—

they listen as if their lives depend on it.
And then they cheer me on.

Beyond the din, I see the blessing
of bluegrass feeding our healthy stock,
fields of hemp and tobacco
reaching toward summer sun.

The dusty air is hot, heavy with the hum
of mosquitoes and drifting clouds of gnats.

I hear the rattle of spoon against fork
as tables are spread with every gift
summer fields and gardens can afford.

I feed on the sight, the sound, the smell of it.
This work is in my blood!

Twice a week I ride the county, stumping
against Uncle Robert, the Whig's candidate.

When he heard I was running, he addressed me
as Brutus—but only in jest. In the South,
thank God, blood is thicker than politics.

We debate the vital issues,
but they do not divide us.

    II.

Uncle Robert supports emancipation.
I, too, the Liberian experiment,
with owners fairly paid for their property

and slaves freed
to set up and rule their own nation.

After much consideration, it is my opinion
that white and black cannot live together.

As tension mounts, the fear on both sides
increases, leading always to violence.

Even at five, I recognized the fear
in the women's eyes when seventy slaves
going down the Ohio with Edward Stone

rose up in Breckinridge County,
the county named after Grandfather.
Armed with wooden billets, axes, and knives,

they killed all four whites, weighted
the bodies, and threw them in the river,
sinking the boat as well.

It always happens in fall.

When apples swelled red on the trees
Grandfather shipped from southern France,
the tension began to build.

That terrible year I was ten,
Nat Turner obeyed his visions.

He said when he prayed, the sun refused to shine,
said the stars guided him,

though others say it was his murdered
master's liquor—a master allegedly kind,

allowing him to preach
the length of Southampton County.

Twenty-four of the sixty
he killed were children.

Star-light, star-bright. . . .
I never again made a wish on a shining star.

The year before little Joseph, our first,
was born, Mary was not well,
large with child. Then we heard about Emily,

nurse for our friend, the abolitionist,
Cassius Clay, who had already freed
several slaves. First one, then the other

of his two young sons took sick and died,
one after nineteen days of vomiting blood.

Arsenic was found in the milk
Emily gave to the little boys.

Mary became hysterical,
beyond any comfort I could give.

She cried that it was wrong
to give this guilty world another child.

After every uprising, the punishment far
outweighs the crime. Public executions—

even women are killed—and good people
converted into beasts hungry for human blood.

Such hatred exists for freedmen,
at the slightest excuse they are lynched,
or beaten and maimed. For the safety
of everyone, we must live in separate nations.

Then we won't dread the harvest,
won't reap slaughter when our leaves
fall orange and red.

Our children can grow up free
of slavery's chains,
its burden of guilt and fear.

This is the end I work toward.

Riding home at night after speaking,
cicadas hidden high above me fiddle
their summer tunes,

owls circle the fields, hunting.

I see lights shining in windows,
human forms moving behind drawn curtains.

A piano's melody reaches out to me
across the darkness, some woman
sitting down at the end of a busy day.

I think of Mary, our three sons,
our daughter, Frances, feel at peace
with myself and the world.

Jacob
THE FOUR SEASONS: WIND

Christmas brings home all
the slaves hired out for a year.
Brings home Master, his wife

and children, and Mistress Laetitia
learns to smile again.

Christmas brings us oranges,
a whole barrelful of gifts given.
Holding them high, the little ones
run till they look like the night

sky full of orange moons. Two weeks
of filled bellies: possum, sweeter
than coon or groundhog, baked slow
with sweet potatoes, skins black
and crisp, hot-orange inside,

and from the big house, molasses
cookies and white taffy we help
pull, and ham, salty and pink.

Mistress leaves the ice house open,
and, sitting in the sawdust, backs
against blocks of river ice,

we drink so much buttermilk,
thick and spotted butter-yellow,
we think we'll turn to gold!

• • •

Mister Will, the overseer, always gives
me chocolate, and I'm polite. If he's
my father, as they say, takes more
than chocolate to make me his son,

after what he did to Easter. Stripped her,
beat her, scarred her face, lied
to Mistress, said she stole from him,

and she's too afraid to tell. He's the one
that stole, and no chocolate candy
will pay back what he took.

When I see him, I keep my fists stuffed
down in my pockets. They want to go
at his face till he's marked up too.

• • •

Snow makes the bare feet cold,
but we pray for snow from the sky,
want everything covered Christmas white.

Field hands off but not the house.
We have parties to serve. When
they sit down, we stand up.

White candles everywhere, the house
shines out like a song. Stars
stop and rest on the cut pine,

just sit there on every branch,
burning like nothing can blow them out.

I think if I could climb
to the top of that tree, wait there
a long time beside that gold
angel, I could learn something
I don't know. I could understand.

Smells from the table trap
your mind on food. Not white folks.
They talk abolition

like it's the Devil come to pull
them under. They watch us serving
like we're the pitchforks and the fire.

But we're the caves they shout into.
And when they shout, we echo.

　　　• • •

Winter wind chases waves
of snow around the barn. Horses
inside stamp, breathe white storms
of steam. Their hooves cut circles
in the snow round as biscuits,

their harness bells ring out
sharp as the icicles hanging
from their furred bellies.

On either side of the road,
trees stand crisp as chitlings.

And there are new mittens, and socks,
and red wool hats, pipe tobacco,
and a polished agate I give
to Master. He says no one

can get the shine out of something
like I can! And a new black cane
for Grampa Sam, and calico cotton,
fine as silk, for Manda, and spices
tied up in a bag with a purple ribbon.

Master gives me shoes. More shoes!
Later, Manda says if shoes were money,
I could buy and free us all!

　　　　　　　　　　　　CIVIL BLOOD

Laughing and crying, we know
we're lucky to be together.

• • •

Three days after Christmas,
we shout in the new year
with Mistress's best whiskey,
and all do the ring dance.

When I have Marcie on my arm,
won't let no-one close to her.
Our feet don't touch the ground,
clapping and beating time

with our feet, others walking around
one by one, until, in the ring, we
do the shout step but never dance
the shout and don't cross feet.

The reds and the blues and the greens
of the women's dresses, the hands
flying through the air to find
each other, the feet we use
to lead us home!

We leave this world, fly
to where there's only step and turn,
only clap and shout, our hearts
chime in our ears like cymbals,

as we forget yesterday, forget
tomorrow, fly to meet our glory!

Then comes New Year's Day,
Heartbreak Day. All those hired out

go back. The quarters fill

with their pitiful crying,
and old Auntie Angel, praying
as she does because she forgets

the words: January, February,
March and April, Lord, Amen,
and this brings in the new year.

Jacob

THIS FOURTH STORY,
I, JACOB, TELL

way back before the first hello, no misery
in this wide world, just people feeding themselves
off the land, food free as all outdoors, and
in those days the land had a voice, and you had
to ask it for food, and it most often said yes
if it was in the mood, and if you talk nice and
respectfully slow 'cause its hearing not so much,
the ears being a ways off: now blue swallow and
catfish and old black bear, they all ask nice
and slow: woman, she takes her time in asking too,
but man, he gets himself busy and forgets once,
forgets twice, forgets one more time until the
land takes back the food that's free: then man
has to break his back for it, fight for it, kill
the bird, kill the bear, but man he's still
moving too fast to see: what am I gonna' get next?
he asks the land, still expecting something and
quick: you gonna' get misery, the land says,
and that's what he gets, and that's what he's got
from that day to this day and on beyond tomorrow

Cabell

MEMORIES OF MY SOUTHERN EDUCATION: JEFFERSON'S FIRST INAUGURAL ADDRESS / IMAGES FROM SLAVERY / KENTUCKY LAW

Jefferson:
All, too, will bear in mind this sacred principle,
that though the will of the majority
is in all cases to prevail, that will to be
rightful must be reasonable; that the minority
possesses their equal rights, which equal law
must protect, and to violate would be oppression.

Images:
Since 1830 we've been a breeding state,
supplying fine horses, mules, hogs,
sheep, and cattle, supplying the Cotton
Kingdom of Mississippi and Louisiana
with hemp to bag and bail their cotton,
supplying them with slaves. Our common
property is approximated at 230,000
slaves, $34,000,000 worth. Before deep snow
and after harvest, you'll meet droves
of hogs, eight-hundred of them going to
Virginia. You'll meet coffles of black cargo
bound for New Orleans or Natchez. They say,
once you've heard, from far away, that terrible
music, you'll never forget it. Chained ankle
and wrist, seventy-five to a hundred wretched
creatures follow behind a black fiddler playing
a lively tune to keep them moving. Under the
Star Spangled Banner, they throw themselves
forward, just ahead of the driver's lash, bare-
foot even in snow. Clumps of ice hang down
from the hems of the women's dresses, drag along
the ground. That grisly music floats up above
the trees: a sprightly fiddler's tune, the rattle
of chains, rough shouts, the crack of a lash,
the moaning.

Jefferson:
Sometimes it is said that man cannot be trusted
with the government of himself. Can he,
then, be trusted with the government of others?
Or have we found angels in the form of kings
to govern him? Let history answer this question.

Images:
Some young whites consider slave watching,
slave hunting, slave catching the best of
sports. The night patrols can enter any slave
cabin, check for passes. It is rumored some
kick the husband out of bed, crawl in
themselves. If a slave runs, after three
calls, a white can shoot him dead; it's best
to bring him back alive so he can take
his punishment, a lesson to himself and to
his fellow slaves. In the northeast corner
of the courthouse yard at Lexington stands
the public whipping post, a three-pronged
poplar tree sunk four feet into solid ground.

Jefferson:
. . . entertaining a due sense of our equal right
to the use of our own faculties, to the acquisitions
of our own industry, to honor and confidence
from our fellow citizens, resulting not from birth
but from our actions and their sense of them;
enlightened by a benign religion, professed
indeed, and practiced in various forms, yet
all of them inculcating honesty, truth,
temperance, gratitude, and the love of man . . .

Law:

Any slave, for rambling in the night or riding
horseback without leave, or running away, may
be punished by whipping, cropping, and branding
in the cheek, or otherwise, not rendering
him unfit for labor.

Jefferson:

acknowledging and adoring an overruling
Providence, which by all its dispensations
proves that it delights in the happiness
of man here and his greater happiness hereafter —
with all these blessings, what more is necessary
to make us a happy and prosperous people?

Law:

Any slave convicted of petty larceny, murder,
or willful burning of dwelling houses
may be sentenced to have his right hand
cut off: to be hanged in the usual manner,
or the head severed from the body, the body
divided into four quarters, and head and
quarters stuck up in the most public place
in the county where such an act was committed.

Jefferson:

Still one more thing, fellow citizens — a wise
and frugal Government, which shall restrain
men from injuring one another, shall leave
them otherwise free to regulate their own pursuits
of industry and improvement, and shall not take
from the mouth of labor the bread it has earned.
This is the sum of good government, and this is
necessary to close the circle of our felicities.

CIVIL BLOOD

Cabell

RUNNING FOR A SECOND TERM
IN CONGRESS: SUMMER 1853

My worthy opponent, Greasy Bob Letcher,
the best Whig vote-getter they've got,

tells funny stories to avoid the issues,
lures the crowd away from my speeches
by playing the fiddle left-handed.

He would laugh and dance them
to his victory
while I discuss, alone, our problems.

And my health not good.

After working three days at a time
without sleep to catch up on correspondence,

I suffer three weeks of illness,
take to my bed to recover,
which puts me behind again,

Manda's tea of sassafras and wild mint
the only remedy strong enough to heal me —
that and the excitement of the stump.

After a meal, the smoke of cigars —
men planning together, giving each other
advice, laughing over shared stories.

I love the camaraderie,
the very *game* of politics!

That's the food that gets my circulation
going — and barbecues, pigs spitted
on green hickory sticks and sizzling

over oak coals, lemonade dipped from barrels
by dusty-bonneted girls to the rustic music
of volunteer firemen in full uniform,

harmony provided by lowing cattle
standing idle under shade trees
or cooling themselves in a nearby stream.

The pressure builds for me to begin
my Presidential bid, but first
I must win this infernal election!

After weeks of Letcher's fiddling,
I begin to boil him in his own
corpulence. He calls me a mere boy,
charges me with once stealing watermelons.

I don't deny the charge, ask any man
who never stole a watermelon to raise
his hand so we can meet a liar.

A hush falls over the crowd —
then laughter.

I bring up his chameleon stance on slavery,
adapting to the mood
of any crowd he addresses,

state again my stand that abolition is
impossible in the South, that the government

has no right to limit or interfere
with slavery whatsoever.

The turning point comes when someone
in the crowd charges Black Bob
with playing left-handed

to hill folk while he plays
with his right for those
in wealthy Bluegrass country.

Then Letcher's notable temper leads him
around by the nose; he calls me a pretty
demagogue, literally foams at the mouth.

Running scared, he's buying votes
in Owen County, paying men twenty dollars
to stay at home and thirty to cast
a Letcher-ous vote.

Although he denies it, the voters know
it's true. Even two jays and a squirrel
come over to my side. They chatter

during my speech, and I charge Letcher
with stooping so low as to bribe

God's innocent creatures
to help him win a losing race!

The glow fades out of him slowly.

Dripping with sweat, wheezing with fury,
he knows and I know
I have him beat.

Jacob
THE FOUR SEASONS: PLOW

Field hands up at four,
chickens clucking and complaining
about it still being dark.

Hands walk slow to the fields
through orchards budding out
with apple and peach and pear.
Don't hardly talk, won't see home

till dark is down again. All day
they stamp the fields of hemp,
pile and burn the empty cases,

dry enough by now to feed
the hunger in a pine-knot torch.

Late night, we see the fires,
smell the smoke, hear their songs

rising sad with the glowing flames
as they walk back slow in twos
and threes from the blazed-out fields.

        . . .

Spring peepers croak all night,
little brown voices of the trees,
when Marcie says she'll be my wife.

Mistress says yes, and Marcie's so happy
she can't hardly see the cotton

she's supposed to card. When Master returns,
Laetitia fixes up an altar under
the catalpa tree, covers a table

white with bed sheets, a pillow
in front for kneeling down upon.

Old Peter Cotton comes to marry us,
his preacher coat sewn high
and mighty with scripture words.

He says the marriage from the Bible,
though he can't read, then says,
You is man and wife
till death or distance do you part.

I put the ring on Marcie's finger,
a ring I've cut out, sanded down
from a big red button I've been saving—
and she cries. Jasmine on the altar

smells almost as sweet as her face is.
When I kiss her, a small wind

shakes the catalpa tree, drops
its white trumpets all around us,

white on the ground, smoke
blowing in from the fields.

Jacob
THIS FIFTH STORY, I, JACOB, TELL

blue swallow has no need of any holiday, every
day's his christmas, every night's his fourth
of july: he takes himself up to the sky, floats
in the blue, held up by the wind's strong hand,
and god sends up his supper: kiri, kiri, kiri,
blue swallow calls out in thanks as god sends up
the mosquito, sends up the moth and black fly:
since god's the one that's made them, he knows
the name of every star, and when he calls, they
sparkle: and god counts every feather on blue
swallow's back, counts even the soft ones on his
belly, and for every feather he gives a blessing:
whoever hurts you, god says, hurts me as well:
you're my love shown to the earth in your flight:
whoever turns away, his seed will blow off in the
wind, his rivers run into the earth, and all his
songs of praise will stick dry in his throat

Jacob
THE FOUR SEASONS: HAY

A summer so hot, we knock out, careful,
the mud daubing from our cabin walls,

eat with the mouse and the wasp
and the occasional cool breeze.

I can't stop looking at Marcie,
tell her she's my summer flower,
and she laughs, pushes me away,

but not too hard, as she pats
corn meal into cakes for the fire.

Her belly's just beginning to swell,
and I sleep with my hand there,
feel my own life moving inside her.

One night I dream blue swallow,
his wings framed gold,
flies from her belly to freedom.

. . .

When the Patterrollers come, two
hold me outside while they

take their time with Marcie. One wears
a silver buckle, the other, who can't stop
smiling, a wooden cross that looks
like he carved it himself. Marcie's cries

mix with the song of the mocking bird
singing the moon from full to thin. . . .
In their own time, they leave.

My two fists ache from squeezing air,
my palms raw where the nails dig in.

When night burns black enough,
I stretch grapevine, green, across
the trail as high as I can reach,

take four Patterrollers off
their running horses by the necks,
not one of them smiling.

Marcie's nights shot full
of holes with screaming,

and the baby, small as a kitten,
comes and goes—a boy.

. . .

To make my mind leave Marcie,
Mister Will takes me to the fights,
watches me like a horse
he's not sure how broke it is.

They put the fight in Brown's orchard,
peach trees all around, fruit ready,

spicing up the hot night.
Old moon full again, circled
faces flicker light and dark

in the flame of raised torches.
Two niggers matched up—Master Brown's
Bill and Master Webb's Sonny. All bet,
cheer for one to kill the other,

but don't really mean it—they'd
both fetch too good a price—just want
one to get the other down.

The two men, big as bears, crouch,
circle each other, moving slow.

Bill closes in first — no knives,
but anything goes. It's clear Sonny's
got no chance, but he fights hard,

uses his head, his hands, his teeth,
bites off part of Bill's right ear,

and Bill, bull mad, gets Sonny's head
in a grip, slashes with his teeth
his right cheek, thumps his head
against his knee, the ground,

and when he lets go, Sonny just
lays there, the men cheering so,
and he don't ever get up,

his cheek split open, white teeth
smiling right on through, smiling,

telling me, Now's the time, boy,
stand on up, take your woman and go.

Jacob
CROSSING OVER

If you'd cross over the great Ohio,
first try to find her frozen, then
remember these names to meet your freedom:
Cairo   Evansville   Leavenworth
They may ride you down first, their dogs
tear off your wet clothes, and when you're
stripped, bend you over a barrel,
Madison   Rising Sun   Lawrenceberg
beat you all over your bare back
with a cobblestone paddle—its forty
holes—every hole drawing its own blister,
Cincinnati   New Richmond   Moscow
and then, the Blacksnake whip, that stiff
handle, three feet of it, like a club,
and the lash, its snake mouth hissing,
Ripley   Manchester   Rome
or a cat-o'-nine tails, each one
doing its own work plowing up your back,
winding around your body, purring,
Portsmouth   Ironton   South Point
but whatever whip they choose,
they'll work it on you till every blister
breaks open, blood running down to your heels,
Burlington   Jeffersonville   Marietta
and then their salt-water wash,
strong enough to float a spoon in,
the salt and the blood and the screaming.
Wellsburg   Steubenville   Point Pleasant
But if you get there, the silence will be yours,
the trees, the earth, and the grass upon it,
the blue blue sky will be yours, all yours.
Proud to meet you, Master Freedom

CIVIL BLOOD

Cabell

VICE PRESIDENT
UNDER BUCHANAN: 1858

I.

I canvassed hard for old Buchanan,

though felt no fondness
for his mediocrity.

Buck and Breck they called our ticket,
wore badges with our names

spelled out in red. I spoke at Tippecanoe,
Hamilton, Kalamazoo, and Pittsburgh.

In Lexington, they trotted out a huge procession,
brass bands and a model ship of state
pulled by thirty-one horses —

fifteen black ones for the slave states
and sixteen white for those they call free.

Mary, our five children, adored
this oom-pah-pah frosting the cake.

Convinced the Republicans meant
to challenge the Union,

my heart was in the race.

With this victory, I was, at thirty-six,
the youngest Vice President,
and, people said, in four years more

the Presidency was mine.

II.

In Ohio, for the first time, men called me
Southerner — as if it were some disease —
and spat upon me. They misunderstand.

Would they allow the government
they elected to take *their* property?

A new mood settles over this nation.
Meaner. Men more willing to fight
than reason together.

With five children to raise I must
give more attention to my law career.

Politics is unpredictable,
and it seems I have
no head for business.

Overinvested in Western land,
I'm forced to sell Malvina,
our last domestic, and her child,
just six weeks old.

We're so fond of her; Malvina
loves our children like her own.

But there's no help for it.

I've found a place for her,
a family who will treat her
with the kindness she's accustomed to.

Yet the parting wrenches us.
We'll miss her sweet ways,

and I fear for her,
knowing I can't affect her fate
beyond this sale.

III.

After we won the election, I found
the President unapproachable, his schedule

fiercely guarded by his niece
who treats me with haughty disdain.

Some call his behavior jealousy,
others a grudge. The more he avoids me,

the more tentative I become, seeking
some lapse in my own behavior.

Settlers name new Western towns for me.
Bloody Kansas gives a whole county my name,
and several unfortunate babies push my
alphabet around before their last names.

Mary loves to have me home. We attend
the appropriate dinner parties,
go to theatre in Alexandria,
the races in Georgetown.

Hostesses choose guest lists
with caution these days. Rival factions
would as willingly exchange bullets
across an elegantly laid table
as biscuits and butter.

Buchanan never consults me on any
affair of state. I preside over
the Senate, break an occasional tie.

Friends from home continue to send
fresh cured hams, Kentucky bourbon.

From so little debate,
I grow fat at the chin.

CIVIL BLOOD

LAETITIA'S MARRIAGE, HER RETURN

We knew it was doomed,
but nothing we did or said would dissuade her.

He made us uneasy, Charles Parkhill,

who loved Laetitia as he loved any
outrageous wager. He fenced with swords,
the guards removed,

considered it sport to race his horse
against any man fool enough

to gallop the woods on a moonless night,
betting his life on the horse and chance alone.

He had her eyes,

wild as something between human and beast,
but on him they resembled more

the falcon's rage held in check
by a taut leather thong

he would break or die.

She was married two years and barely
a word from her. Although she looked

unwell, whenever I inquired
after her health,

she averted her eyes, said nothing.

When I voiced my concern, Mother said
Parkhill must be taming her,
a job no one could envy,

and we laughed. In two years Parkhill
suddenly died, and Laetitia returned home—

at least some part of her returned.

She walked the woods at night
calling his name, calling my name.

Jacob found her curled asleep on the Indian mound—
even to him she was lost,
and I, in Washington City, too far away to help.

Her hair turned white, she aged twenty years in two,
and when we buried her,

the women preparing the body found, upon her stomach
and breasts, tiny scars, healed cuts
from the tip of an unguarded sword. How often

I have killed, in my mind,

that dead man, slowly.

Cabell

RUNNING FOR PRESIDENT AGAINST LINCOLN, DOUGLAS, AND BELL: 1860

I.

Now that it's dark, our children celebrate
the Fourth of July. It's ironic to watch
them reenact our independence.

They light fireworks imported from China,
shoot the tiny cannon with its puff of smoke,

beat their drums, chasing out the British
once again. Little Mary, the youngest,
always plays the colonial role.

She runs on stocky legs,
the rest after her, holding back,
pretending full speed.

Soon they'll catch her, and we'll warn,
as we do each year, Not too rough now.

Rushing to grow up, they
would try out the violence
perfected by adults.

At the annual fireworks and parade,
the sky's dark garden bloomed
with flowers that quickly faded.

Bands played, their brassy cheer
dulled by foreboding.

Surrounded by women and children,
men watching the parade
carried guns or brass knuckles —

didn't even try to hide them!

Under the torches held high,
their faces looked demented—

I felt myself shudder.

This world's become a breeding ground
for sneers and insults,

threats upon my life.

The foot can so easily slip,
the heart refuse to beat.

Any lunatic can seek you out,

label you the cause of his misfortune,
dispense his own brand of justice.

Yesterday, a group of Senators, men
from North and South, who once delighted
in my company, groaned as I approached,

Northerners no doubt sickened
by my pleas for equal treatment

of our smaller South,
Southerners, more hot-headed

than wise, disgusted with my demands
for peaceful solutions.

II.

I began my political life pledging
compensation for any owner freeing

his black property, end it
demanding our government
protect his investment.

I run against Lincoln, husband
of my childhood friend, Mary Todd.
He's a good man, ungainly but bright.

Fortune must be having a hard laugh.

After years of dedicated service,
the Presidency in sight,
this world's inescapable evil

pushes me off a safe road
into that swamp
between desire and realization.

There's no firm ground.

III.

I give speeches, more speeches,
this ceremony of words chalked
on the blackboard of futility.

Not that my convictions
have changed—it's just the eyes
in mirrors. This face they call fair
is nothing more substantial than glass

reflecting a man's obscure outline—

his look is serious or that eternal
smile—frozen like a tintype.

And when I open my mouth to sing,
streamers fly out—red, white
and blue. They add a comic touch,

accompanying the patriotic songs
I hear myself singing,

caught in the act of staying alive.

Cabell
THE ELECTION OF 1860

Life becomes a solid wall
of agony, a nightmare repeating itself

in daylight scene by scene, predicted.

It is I who announce,
voice echoing through the Senate chambers,

Abraham Lincoln is duly elected
President of these United States.

I have smiled too much.

My face, from false congratulations, aches.
Presiding over the Senate, I note

every coat bulging with weapons,
pledges of peace transformed into bullets.

Hatred poisons whatever it touches.

Like a sickness, it must be leeched,
but not by spilling a neighbor's blood.

I hear my own voice, its hollow ring
floating far away from me,

Abraham Lincoln is duly elected
President of these United States.

The election was a rout.

Even Kentucky turned against me.

One by one, the Southern states follow
South Carolina from the Union.

Fort Sumter is fired upon.

The Senate's fool, I urge reconciliation
long beyond its feasibility.

General Winfield Scott surrounds
with Federal troops the House chambers.

John Brown killed to be crowned hero.

And now, the Northern press invites
the black South to rise up, complete,

with butchery, this lunatic beginning.
Before Brown was hanged,

he said our nation's guilt
must be washed away with blood.

The North agrees. Don't they know,
the blood he means is *our* blood?

I mourn what might have been.
Papers that called me Glorious
change my name to Traitor.

My voice, some parody of doom, announces,

Abraham Lincoln is duly elected
President of these United States.

Tradition is a soiled rag,
fit to wipe a sword with.

Our son, Cabell, runs away
to Tennessee. Just sixteen, he lies
about his age, joins the Confederacy.

In Lexington, Uncle Robert leads
the Union volunteers to Fort Sumter.

Against this muster of troops, this clatter
of rifles, I quote the Constitution

until I hear the Federals
are coming to arrest me.

I couldn't make them understand:
Our enemy is *war*, not one another.

Honor demands I fight,
though the Southern cause

is utterly without hope.

I pack a small valise,
say farewell

to Mary and the children. Her blue satin
dress is laid out on the bed for a wedding
we never attend. Seeing it there,

I feel so weary.

Warned by their mother not to cry,
the children stand bravely in a row
to wave good-bye.

Turning my horse toward Tennessee,

I am the one who weeps.

Jacob
THE FOUR SEASONS: HARVEST

Every slave shack's boasting strings
of shucky beans, red peppers,
run to jesus, shun the danger
I know the other world's not like this
and harvest corn, every rooftop's busy
drying peach and apple pies.
I won't stay much longer here
I know the other world's not like this
Old moon is full for the all night
corn shucking at Master Webb's,
run, sister, run, run, sister, run
I know the other world's not like this
a fire as high as a two-storied
house is burning red, then gold,
fire in the east, fire in the west
I know the other world's not like this
burning purple and blue. Faces
dancing wildly in the heat of flame,
you're going to reap just what you sow
I know the other world's not like this
alive with laughter, our songs of hope
sung out at the top of our lungs to the night,
I call myself a child of god
I know the other world's not like this
pig turning 'round on the spit,
shucked corn cool in your hands,
walk away, children, don't get weary
I know the other world's not like this
unless you find a red one—
then you get a swig of brandy,
up on the mountain, down in the valley
I know the other world's not like this
get to kiss any girl on the place.
I kiss Marcie, her skirt bulging
heaven is my rightful home
I know the other world's not like this
with pone cakes, dried apples, a blanket.

Tonight is the night we're going to run—
tell jesus done, done all I can
I know the other world's not like this
so when the moon helps us out,
hides its face behind a cloud,
slavery chains are broke at last
I know the other world's not like this
we crouch down, then run,
head north toward the wide Ohio and freedom.
a child of god, I'm on my way
I know the other world's not like this
Grampa Sam drew maps in the dirt
but night eats up remembering.
a long long time, I'm on my way
I know the other world's not like this
We run from bush to ditch to tree
singing softly to chase our fear.
my bones are aching, racked with pain
I know the other world's not like this
Twice, by full moon, I see
Sonny grinning his white grin.
I'm going to praise god till I die
I know the other world's not like this
Fire left behind, the hand of night
closes its fist around us.
meet me on that other shore
I know the other world's not like this

Jacob
THIS LAST STORY, I, JACOB, TELL

blue swallow and his mate drift in a red-sun
sky, greet what the wind brings: they dip low
to the earth, spy a pack of hounds, hear men's
voices call out again and again, so they flap
their wings, fly toward the clouds, as one shot
cracks the sky: blue swallow's mate jerks upward,
then falls like a blue stone, falls slow through
the dark pool of her own shadow, lies still
in the clearing: blue swallow circles and circles,
crying out to her, kiri, kiri, kiri: old wind woman
answers in her sad and lonely way, sending him
a warning too cold to understand: swooping down
to his mate, blue swallow hops up close enough to
know that old man death has her for his own: the
sorrow is so mighty, blue swallow can hardly move,
but he hears the hounds nearby, spreads his wings,
feels a net fall over and around him, pin him
to the ground, the sound of dogs upon him,
howling fit to kill howling fit to kill howling

THE BATTLE
II

General John Cabell Breckinridge
MY RECURRING DREAM:
DECEMBER 2, 1862

Every night I dream we're fighting, armies raised
high to celestial fields flooded with lunar light.
Up in the sky, everything moves faster in the mercury
of air. The armies step across clouds, brisker than
before, heaviness gone from their feet. Then the
firing begins; one shot, and the white sky crumbles.
A cough, a sigh float across the field. The drummer
boy is fiercely drumming as a big man carries him
across the stream. Bayonets sparkle like winter stars.
The armies advance, blue and gray, December wind punishing
every inch of skin. No blood stains red this nightly war,
fought in black and white. A harvest moon shines on the
jumble of mangled forms. Stands of grass bend and dry
before they burn. A soldier has found his left foot
hiding inside his boot; one gropes for his head, but it
has rolled away. Another limps, using his gun as a crutch.
When fire starts up in the field, the wounded call for help.
Now they're begging. Shells pop like fireworks to punctuate
their screams. I carry wounded men from the field, stumble
and fall, flames raging closer. Face stinging from the heat,
I smell my mustache burning, run, flames surrounding me,
wake thrashing, wet with perspiration. Rising alone, I
build up the fire, heat some water for coffee to rinse
the taste of gunpowder and smoke from my mouth.

CIVIL BLOOD

INTRODUCING GENERAL BRAXTON BRAGG, COMMANDER OF THE CONFEDERATE ARMY OF TENNESSEE

In her Edmonton Diary, Mrs. Katharine Ann Devereaux wrote, "He was an unhappy man . . . he had an unhappy birth." As his mother panted, the final fist of childbirth squeezing her, his head crowned, then emerged. His tiny mouth, blood-smeared and crying, was twisted into the tense, worried expression that never left him.

In one version, he was born in jail, his pregnant mother behind bars for shooting and killing an uppity black. She screamed at the jailer to run fetch her husband quick! His father, a local carpenter, rushing from his work on the exclusive girls' school that would lift the family high enough to glimpse respectability, didn't make it in time for the birth.

Another version says the baby arrived at home, shortly after his mother's release from jail.

This story his mother told him: At the lavish annual Christmas party given by the large tobacco planters, one young woman, the wealthy Buehl's only daughter, refused to dance with Joe Masters, the butcher's son. The young Miss Buehl looked at his rough red hands, horrified, stepping back. Evidently she let out a little scream just to think that nothin' Joe would presume to ask a lady to dance. His mother stressed the word *lady*, then went back to her wash.

As a child, Bragg had several collections. He treasured white rocks starred with shining mica, arranged them in order of size, small to large. He never forgot a tragic or gruesome story: How vultures and rats slowly devoured a slave hung up live in the swamp, the one accused of raping that white woman from Deer Hollow. On full moon nights, his cries could still be heard.

Bragg never harmed a living thing. Couldn't stand even to
put a worm on a hook, but he collected the feet of dead
animals. A single crow, rabbit, sparrow, and racoon foot
rested on his shelf, their movement slowed to that of the
stones they rested between.

When he was five years old, the town children began to call
him hound-face. Because he cried, the nickname stuck.
His health, never good, became more fragile. At the
slightest provocation, he suffered nausea, and, if forced
to eat, vomited immediately. Attacks of boils plagued him
and migraine headaches so severe he staggered when he walked,
had to be put to bed.

There he dreamed his recurring dream: As the uniformed
drum corps played staccato drum rolls, he rode up to the
town square on a white stallion, nostrils flaring red.
Off in the distance, a cannon fired twenty-one slow times
as he presented his prizes, one by one, to the most beautiful
girl in Warrenton. Wearing a ruffled white dress, she stood
with her back to him as he placed, beside her white satin
shoes, twenty-one bloodied enemy gloves. She never turned
toward him. He never saw her face.

Uncoordinated by nature, he climbed from the pasture fence
back up on his father's plow mare time after time, crying
bitterly, snotty blood dangling from his nose and chin,
until he finally learned to ride. He was known as an
excellent horseman.

At seven he was sent to Warrenton Male Academy where he was
remembered by his teachers as bright, attentive, anxious
to please. He wanted to be either a lawyer or an architect
like his brothers. When he was ten, his parents decided
on his career: Since he seemed so military minded, he would
be a soldier. Although his father was newly risen from a

carpenter to a successful contractor who owned five slaves,
he was short of money because of the older boys' college
expenses. Through his political connections, he procured
for young Bragg an appointment to West Point which was free.

Once there, the boy did well in his studies, easily able to
learn a text and say it back on command. Other than school
assignments, he never read. Developing a lifelong talent
for making enemies, he saw people as best friends or bitter
foes, saw answers as right or wrong. Besides schoolwork,
he learned to march, handle and fire a weapon, stand guard,
and dance. To learn dancing, the young cadets paired off
with one another. He was always last to be chosen. One
classmate remembered him as generous, brave, and clever.
Another as uncouth, brusque, and rude.

When he began West Point, he never touched liquor, but
his sour disposition made him the butt of countless jokes.
Toward the end of his freshman year, he decided to learn
to drink. Buying a bottle of good Kentucky bourbon,
he sneaked away on one of the first warm Sundays in May
and sat by the river to instruct himself. Lying on his
back in the grass, he watched the sky, slightly overcast,
through the darkened green-lace curtain of new leaves.
He was joined by a big hound, tongue lolling out from
a recent hunt. He patted the dog, offered it a drink,
which it refused, then finished the bottle himself, gulping
down the warm liquid without tasting it, not waiting for
one swallow to work its devilment before taking another.

Hours later, at dusk, he woke throwing up. It was raining.
Naked except for black stockings, he found his uniform next
to him, neatly folded, boots beneath it, raising it above
the dirt. And, on the other side of him, the dog lay still,
pink tongue stretched out, crawling with black ants. Shiver-
ing, he hurriedly put on his uniform, damp from the rain, but

clean. As he lifted the dog—how heavy it was—the head
swung wildly from its broken neck. After he released it
to the river and watched it swirl away in the spring current,
he rinsed out his mouth and washed his face and hands long
and slow in the cold water. Then he sat staring at his
hands, palms up, until it was nearly dark. By the time
he returned to school, both hands had erupted in boils.
He went right to bed, desperately sick for a week, was given
demerits, confined to campus for leaving without permission.
But he never complained. For over two months he couldn't
write, carry or fire a weapon, wear gloves. He never drank
another drop of liquor, not even wine with dinner, and the
smell of bourbon on someone's breath made him reel with
nausea and clutch nervously, one hand for the other.

Just before he graduated from West Point, he told a classmate
that he prided himself on being the ugliest man in the corps.

Although he was determined, his determination was blind.
Devoid of imagination and humor, he made life itself a
laborious duty. He punished others ruthlessly for his own
imperfection. And if he'd made up his mind, no amount of
reason could persuade him to change his course of action.
If things didn't turn out as he planned, he became confused,
the victim of such severe migraines he couldn't think at all.

Although harsh, he was usually fair. Often however, his
single-mindedness worked against him, and he blamed others,
appeared to believe even the most ridiculous charges.

Nothing he did was unstudied. Nothing came easily. Over-
scrupulous, he planned entire conversations in his mind.
What they would say, what he would say, what they would say,
what he would say. In the best of these rehearsed dialogues,
his smile was wooden, his words stilted. Caught off guard,
without preparation, he couldn't force even a small grin,

managed to say exactly the wrong thing. If another person's greatest shame was being overweight, fat would immediately force its way into the conversation, refuse to leave; talking about a certain cannon, for example, he would use the phrase "fat as a hog" to describe it, then watch astounded while the conversation disappeared into a terrible silence.

Uneasy with women, he seldom courted. No one, including himself, could understand how he was able to win such a prize for a wife. He could never believe his good fortune. Elise Bragg was not only beautiful, intelligent, and wealthy, but she also adored him. It was a love match. She wrote a good friend shortly after their marriage that he was as tender and loving a husband as any woman could dream of. Their devotion deepened, year by year, their rich relationship undiluted by children. She was the perfect mate for him. When he couldn't think, she thought for him. When he couldn't speak, she spoke for him.

And so it was he prepared to become General Braxton Bragg, who, under a large sycamore tree in Tennessee, would order General John Cabell Breckinridge, against all good advice, to run his men elbow to elbow across Stones River and take the occupied hill, would order them to run uphill toward sixty cannon, so that in a matter of minutes hundreds of them would lie dead or maimed, as the rest retreated under relentless fire across the cold and bloody river.

General John Cabell Breckinridge
DECEMBER 4, 1862:
FIRST SNOW, MURFREESBORO

We ride on a tree-lined path toward Stones River.
Winter, leaves soft under our horses' hooves,
gold leaves, gold as the wood of a fine table.
This path stretches before us as if we could
walk on gold forever. Snow begins falling,
first snow, falling slowly, the day windless,
each large and intricate flake appearing
to fall up, fall back toward the gray magnet
of sky. Overhead, trees touch branches, inter-
lace, forming a steeple roof above our heads,
an arch that allows the light. Ahead, golden
fields, tall grass pressed flat by last night's
camping troops, leafless bushes scattered
for accent through the field, dotted red as
Mary's embroidery stitches, then brakes of
dense cedar, ominous shadows. On the far side
of the field, beyond our camp, we cross Stones
River on planks hastily laid for wagons hauling
cannon. The water is so clear. On the muddy
river bottom, brown leaves line this restless
sky sunk in the earth, brown leaves moving
slowly in the water as if touched by a dream
of breeze. Snow falls thickly at a slant.
On the path beyond the river, trees give way
to gnarled bushes, their branches reaching out,
forming above our heads an ominous brambled roof.
Too low for us to ride beneath, we dismount,
lead our horses through, snow blanketing
with white every saddle, every hat and shoulder.
Destroying the silence, ending our peaceful
thoughts, we hear from far away the unnatural
sound of thunder made by human hands. Snow
falls in wet flakes, covering our footprints.

Jacob
DECEMBER 8, 1862: MURFREESBORO

(i)

When the patrol brings me back, legs
nearly chewed off by those hounds,
I promise Mistress never to try

escape again if she lets me go
with Master. Besides, I say, how'll
he survive without me in the war?

When she refuses, I tell her, Shoot me
then, just shoot me. I lost
Marcie, and Laetitia's gone, and now,

he is all I got, and if I'm no good
to him, just do me the same respect

you do a dog and put a bullet
through my head and call it finished.

(ii)

So I go to him, do my best
to save his life — and likewise for
myself. Have never seen at one time

so many dead as this war makes.
After the guns shut up, all night

black and white boys walk among
the dead and dying holding candles.
You see those little flames

flicker through the fields for miles.
They lean over, calling out a name,
hoping not to see that dead one

is their Master or best friend.
Those the saddest lights
I ever hope to see.

(iii)

When the bullets come up close,
I drop on the ground, cheer them on:

Keep on coming! Over here!
We sure are ready, Master Lincoln!

But not out loud. I want my freedom,
long as they don't hurt my Master.

If those Yankees draw a gun on him,
they have to shoot me first.

(iv)

I take good care of my favorite flea,
call him Wild Man Flash,

'cause he's the fastest flea in camp.
Put a candle under a tin plate,

can't nothin' hold him back.

I win some gloves, fleece-lined,
trade those gloves and a pair
of red shoes for a book,

hide that book under my blanket,
read when everyone's asleep.

(v)

I do anything to make Master laugh.
Such sadness hides behind his eyes.

What's one flea say to another?

I ask him, and when he gives up,
tell him the answer:

Shall we walk or ride a dog?

I save spirits for him to fight off
the morning chill, put Wild Man Flash

on a tin plate, win easy a chicken
I fix up for his supper. Don't ever

tell him I gamble. He's dead set
against the sin of it. Don't tell him,

too, the chicken's stolen.

General John Cabell Breckinridge
MY WIFE'S VISIT TO MURFREESBORO:
DECEMBER 12, 1862

Across December's landscape,
our wives, in black carriages,

arrive, followed by teams
of mules pulling wagons,

canvas covers bulging
with supplies: Christmas
cookies, fruitcakes,

fat turkeys, just killed
and stored on ice, cranberries,
wine, brandy, and blankets,

letters from worried families,
and any medicine our wives
could buy or beg.

When I first see Mary,
I feel like a boy,
sixteen again, stammering.

We camp in a cotton field
with the other officers
and their wives,

walk holding hands,

crunch across plants
spilling cotton from

brittle pods over earth
dusted with snow.

Mary sews for the wounded,
nurses them, cutting off

their torn clothing,
stained red and frozen
to their gaping wounds,

holds cups to their
cracked lips, tucks
blankets around them

to still the shivering
a blanket can't still.

Even the young ones look old.

Late at night, darkness added
to their suffering,

they lie engulfed
in the loneliness of men
wounded back to little boys.

Their sunken eyes,
search her face for
answers she can't provide.

They call out pitifully
to her, saying they know
they'll pull through

if she'll nurse them,
and she comes,

changes their bandages,
cools their fevers
with a damp cloth,

holds their hands as,
one by one, they die,

her calm presence
escorting them
into the unknown.

At day's end, depleted sun
dropped behind the remains
of trees, her eyes are

as hollow as theirs.
I hold her until she weeps,
shuddering from the agony
she's absorbed.

She searches my face
for the balance of life
and death I carry there.

We build our fire up higher.

Cotton pods rattle
as ghosts hover around us
in the fields.

She thinks she hears her name
called out. And then again.

Later she dreams I'm shot,
lying alone in the field
as fall leaves gradually

cover me, that mound
whitening with snow.

CIVIL BLOOD

I wake when she touches my face,
hold her as she cries again.

She worries about not being near
if I should be wounded,
worries that no one will find me,

nearly raves about infection,
the importance of warm food.

I hush her in my arms.

Death brings our fragile bodies
closer. Before we sleep,

we share one more thought,
and then, another. . . .

Tonight, all we are
we can accept:
alive, together.

OFFICERS' CHRISTMAS PARTY:
MURFREESBORO

The Town Hall shimmers with the light of hundreds
of white candles, flames reflected from the polished
bayonets behind them, walls brushed by the flight
of angel wings.
        Flowers, carefully tended, bloom
on every table — poinsettias, roses, carnations — their dense
perfume mingling with freshly grated cinnamon and cloves.

On one wall, pine garlands form the letters B and B, entwined.
Bragg and Breckinridge dance in circles with their wives as
if they're alone on the dance floor, their white-gloved hands

flat across their wives' backs, leading;
the lace-covered hands of the women rest across the gold
stars encircling their husbands' necks.

So many hands in the room, hands clapping, waving,
smoothing down a skirt, guiding slaves with heaping
platters of sweet potatoes, rice pudding,

a black hand putting a fallen red rose back in the vase,
sucking the drop of blood from a pricked finger, shaping
the mound of rice with a silver spoon, wiping a buttered
thumb onto a white apron,
        all of those individual hands,
each separate finger, this infinite human flutter!

Spread across one wall, remnants of Federal flags
captured by General Morgan. Most are jaggedly ripped and
bloody, the artwork of brute force.
        The buffet table steams,
succulent with cashews and salmon, with turkey and ham,
a winter rainbow of vegetables and pies —

fruit sliced and sugared by practiced black hands,
crusts oozing apples and peaches from cut-out
crescent moons and stars.

Violins play as uniformed officers whirl their wives
around the hall.
Elise Bragg captures her General's complete
attention when she speaks, then laughs at something he says
in response. As he pulls her closer, she puts her cheek
next to his, closes her eyes.

Mary Breckinridge listens,
enraptured, to her handsome husband, whispers in his ear,
asking him in her sweetest voice, please, not to have another
drink, and he laughs as if she hasn't spoken.

These two women have sent letters beginning, "My Dear
One" or "Beloved." Often the letters go on too long.

Neither woman shows any sign of strain
tonight, happy to whirl among the white candles,

whirl on the wings of the dance, united at last—
is it only a dream?—with their husbands.
If only the party
would never end—music and the smell of cinnamon, pine trees
dressed in colored lanterns, the shimmer of light,
flags captured in victory. . . .

Just beyond the flickering walls, soldiers sit, grouped
around campfires warming themselves. Some talk,
some read, others, with sticks,

dry socks or boots over smoky flames, listen to the rising
song of violins. One man reads a letter,

another stares at the sky as if the stars could comfort him.
Beyond these rings of firelight, the silent fields,
waiting, and darkness.

NASHVILLE: DECEMBER 1862

Beyond the rings of firelight at Murfreesboro, beyond
the rows of tents, the horses, tethered, dozing, lies
Nashville, occupied by Federal troops. Nashville,
formerly pride of the South, now a wound, suppurated,
oozing. The rumor spreads quickly, first whispered by
one Federal officer to another. Within two days every
occupying soldier has heard it. At the Murfreesboro
Christmas party, how they carefully spread the United
States' flag on the floor, then took turns spinning
upon it, Bragg and Breckinridge leading the dance.

Nashville, the Southern city that always led the way,
first to shed the light of education, free, upon its
citizenry. Now there's a nine o'clock curfew. Not
that it helps. North Front Street, once housing two
hundred prostitutes, overflows with fifteen hundred.
They sleep and work three or four to a single room.
One girl, fresh from the farm, no money and no friends,
arranges her straw and blankets in a broom closet, then
goes out looking for business. Soon these women will be
rounded up—some crying, some cursing—their few belongings
wrapped in scarves or sheets or tattered suitcases tied
hastily shut, rounded up and shipped in packed boxcars to
Louisville, told not to come back. But they come back.

The prostitutes return, one by one, two by two, because
their families are slowly starving. Starvation creeps
across the South like a shadow, steadily moving, covering
the cities first. Children's shoes cost over fifteen
dollars a pair, a barrel of flour, fifty-five, a can of
sardines, once five cents, is now five dollars. Mobs of
starving women riot in Atlanta, Mobile, and Richmond.
In Nashville, a baker's throat is cut; he dies before
the bleeding can be stopped. No one is arrested,
although witnesses say a woman did it with a broken
bottle because, even when she told him her children
were starving, he refused to give her three hard rolls.

The war, about to enter its third year, has killed
and maimed thousands. In every public place, men
learn to live without fingers, an arm or a leg—
and these are only the visible wounds. Across the
South, demented people wander. Most of them are women
wounded by war, women who have fed their husbands
and sons, who have fed their babies to war's insatiable
hunger. Some of these women follow the soldiers from
one camp to another. Officers warn of disease, forbid
their men to visit them, but the warnings are ignored.

The soldiers call one of these women Blue Ribbon Rosie
because she ties blue ribbons in her hair. Her unwashed
face oily with grime, wearing layers of dirty rags, she
scavenges around the soldiers' camp. No matter how many
times they remove her from the battlefield, she returns
for every battle. Amidst the masses of uniformed and
moving men, flags of every color, the glint of metal,
shells erupting like volcanoes as they shatter the earth,
throwing up dirt and black clouds of smoke, they see her
stepping between the dead and dying like some carrion bird,
pecking her crooked way across the battlefield, moving
toward some destination she cannot comprehend.

In Nashville, only the theatre seems to have benefitted.
Every day the *Nashville Dispatch* prints the name of the
evening's performance: names like *Cotillion Manor,
Justice Triumphant*, and *Jonathan Whitecastle's Return*.
The paper states that crowds are large and responsive
even in poor weather, urges the purchase of tickets in
advance, or early arrival to guarantee a place in the full
houses. Night after night, preceded by drum rolls,
the plays go on, audiences hushed, starving for fiction.

Blue Ribbon Rosie (i)

yesterday or tomorrow
when I was young
they called me pretty

spare the stick
spare the child

I walked in the woods
imagined a life filled
with more than work

moon in my hands
fire in my heart

the oldest of ten
I sang as I scrubbed
the little ones

all gone   gone
up in smoke

hummed as I washed
and mended their clothes

god's terrible fire
will scorch your brow
burn your face

told them stories
of castles and princes
in faraway lands

even water cannot
kill that fire
burning inside

dreamed of the man
who would take me away
from our dusty farm

only memory
will not burn

ONE SIDE OF THE CONVERSATION BETWEEN GENERAL JOHN CABELL BRECKINRIDGE AND COMMANDER BRAXTON BRAGG: EVENING, CHRISTMAS DAY, 1862

General Breckinridge: General Bragg, I come to you
requesting the life of Asa Lewis which you alone
can spare. I come to plead for mercy. . . .

. . .

General Breckinridge: But you know the circumstances, Sir.
His father's untimely death, his mother too sick to farm. . . .

Please hear me out. These boys are like my own, and Asa
one of the best — honest, distinguished in his bravery
at bloody Shiloh. He's earned the love of all. . . .

. . .

General Breckinridge: Yes, he did desert twice, and
twice caught and returned. But it's Christmas, his mother
wrote she needed him, would die in peace if she could only. . . .

. . .

General Breckinridge: Sir, Kentucky men are different —
volunteers not regular soldiers. I need not remind you

their state is Union. Though his enlistment was up
in December, Asa stayed on, planned to return again.
To execute him the day after Christmas. The men. . . .

. . .

General Breckinridge: Please let me finish. They say
you hate those men from Tennessee, Kentucky, say your

wife urges you to put them in the front so your other
troops can shoot the cowards down if they should run.

For your own sake, for the common good, I beg you, pardon
this decent man, this fine soldier. . . .

. . .

General Breckinridge: I know about the rules, the high
desertion rate, but it's Christmas, we swim in mud,

no boots or coats. And if you lose their love — not love —
respect, I mean, the men won't gladly die. . . .

THE BATTLE

WILL SOMMERS, CONFEDERATE SOLDIER, SPEAKS OF THE EXECUTION: MORNING, DECEMBER 26, 1862

ORDER FROM COMMANDER BRAGG:

The said Asa Lewis will be executed by shooting
in the presence of the troops of the brigade
to which he belongs on December 26 between
ten in the morning and two in the afternoon.

as they buried him, momentarily,
the clouds parted,
we saw a rainbow, cheered

knowing my prayer
was answered, knowing my gun
held the blank, I both cried
and laughed at once

the men, rightfully concerned,
tried to give me liquor, which,

sick at heart, I could not drink

I am chosen for the firing squad. Asa, my friend, sits
waiting in his cell, waiting my gun—blank or ball.

all aimed for the heart,
he fell, thunder,
then torrential rain

It is said our beloved General Breckinridge sat through
the night with him; by morning, became his father, he,
the son. It is said the stars refused to shine.

PART OF ASA LEWIS'S LAST LETTER:

Mother, I would have preferred
a different death and honorable,
but beg you not to feel ashamed. . . .

My comrades think I've done no wrong,
snuffed out, an example, by General Bragg.

I have given my personal effects
to General Breckinridge. He will return
them to you when this war is over.

My greatest fear is that, out of love,
the squad will not shoot with accuracy.

The last unjustly killed deserter —
it took three rounds to quiet him —
how he suffered, calling out to friends. . . .

eleven guns, one blank,
sounded across the meadow
as loud as any battle

This morning, the officers, together in a tense group,
went to Bragg again to ask for mercy, and, again,

he refused, wouldn't even listen, said he'd kill
every last soldier from Kentucky if he must, to teach
them how to follow orders. And that was all.

we marched behind the lead wagon
trying not to see his face,
the glaze of his eyes

Our General flew at Bragg shouting we Kentuckians
would not be killed like cattle. He was barely
able to be restrained.

JACOB SPEAKS:

That old Bragg, he's a stranger
to kindness. You introduce kindness
to him, he won't hold out his hand.
Just turn his back and walk away.

THE BATTLE

breakfast was stale hardtack
and cold coffee. we huddled
in smoky circles, shivering

Several officers planned to return to Bragg with loaded
guns, but the General restrained them; three Lieutenants
refused command of the squad.

we tried to start our breakfast
fires in rain. they smoked,
sputtered, gave off little heat

This is how it is accomplished: The prisoner rides
in the first wagon, a guard to the right, a guard
to the left. In the next wagon, newly cut and nailed,

the coffin. Then officers on horseback followed by
the marching twelve-man firing squad. They stack

their guns, then march away. The guns are loaded—
eleven balls, one blank. (How I prayed that day!)

General Breckinridge dismounted, walked up to Asa.
They spoke for a moment, voices hushed. Then, walking
slowly, he returned to his horse.

THE LAST WORDS OF ASA LEWIS:

I'd choose to have my eyes uncovered
but know it's easier on you men who

have drawn this unhappy job if I am masked,
and so be it. I make but one request:

Comrades, I know you are all grieved
to do this work, but do not be distressed.
None of you will know who kills me.

Each man may think his was the harmless gun.

But I beg of you—aim to kill
when the command, *Fire*, is given.

It will be merciful to me. Good-bye.

WILL SOMMERS' PRAYER / THE SHOUTED COMMANDS:

Lord, let my gun be
that which holds the blank,
and I swear

 Ready . . .

I'll never again
fire a gun to end
a human life

 Aim . . .

even if I must die
myself to keep
this solemn vow.

 Fire!

Asa, friend, may your soul
rest in peace, and mine,
too, if it is willed.

*early on, the blue sky
clouded over, not a single
morning bird was singing*

General Breckinridge, at the order, *Fire*, pitched
forward on his horse's neck, was held astride
by the men around him.

Blue Ribbon Rosie (ii)

my father was too poor
to feed us   so he
arranged my marriage

   angels whispered some
   name at my back

to a farmer older
even than himself

   circles chasing
   themselves   running
   around in circles

what my husband
lacked in money

he made up for
in words

   when they light the cannon
   the sun begins to scream

but a good man

he didn't deserve
what he got

   mountains of flowers
   belch forth from the earth

two babies came
almost at once

   the children shall suffer
   and come unto me

   I don't understand
   the question

General Braxton Bragg
DECEMBER 30, 1862: THE NIGHT BEFORE
THE BATTLE—AFTER BRECKINRIDGE LEAVES
HIS TENT

There is such a thing as
too much beauty in a man—

something in his eyes . . .
what they know . . . dark

blue, yet strangely lit.
Sending politicians

to win a bloody war
with handshakes and smiles!

Tell me, General, the distance
your pretty smile will carry

a shell. And how many boys
have your eloquent speeches saved?

He claims his scouts uncovered
sixty cannon hidden

beyond the crest of hill.
I smelled, on his breath, liquor!

Out! I finally shouted.
You know that this is war,

you know that some must die—
and then some more. The guns

don't take a vote. It's all
in numbers. They *must advance,*

waves of moving flesh
muffling that cannon roar.

You will attack tomorrow.
My order's final. Boys

or not, they're here to fight,
and you will send them in.

That smell again. Liquor!
I'm sure I saw him lurch,

overcome with tears.
Tender as a woman!

Elise, wife, my battered
heart's better half,

I need you here tonight
to help me sort my thoughts,

lay them side by side
like colored strands of yarn

and find some pattern there. . . .
Breckinridge might call

upon his lineage to trip
the legs of Yankee bullets.

Will Sommers, Confederate Soldier
DECEMBER 30, 1862: THE NIGHT BEFORE THE BATTLE HE PREPARES TO FIGHT, GUN NOT LOADED

To have risen before the black rooster,
myself crowing in the new day, to have heard
the chorus of wild birds blessing the dew
on my land, to have sunk my hands up to the wrists
in dirt, dark and warm as inside of a cow,
reaching for the turned strangling head of her new one,
to have touched the silky tassel of wheat, golden,
the newly shorn rug of a sheep's back,
the white oak plank I've sanded smooth,
soft as the inside of a woman's elbow,
stroked the underwater skin of catfish, cool
and dark, that surprise of spines, to have dropped
seed into holes I alone made, firmed
warm earth down around them, to have witnessed
the first green shoots, threads of life
so strong in their push for sun they cracked
apart the earth, to have fought squirrel, crow,
rabbit, drought, army worm, drought,
weevil, flood, despair, Hessian fly,
grasshopper, blight, cankerworm, despair,
to keep new life alive, to have watched the green
blades of young corn curl under,
brown like brittle fodder in the scorch of sun,
to have mourned the hay rotting on the ground in rain,
to have held the still warm calf I could not save,
shot the delicate bay mare
mired in the mud hole, half eaten by wild boar,
to have smelled my wife's hair, long
and darkly sweet, new washed, drying in the sun,
to have caught, with my rough hands, a daughter,
then two sons and held them, heard them, slippery
red, cry out their first hellos, to have built
a tiny box from the old cedar, buried a girl,
fist no bigger than a plum,
to have watched my wife's face, a full year

vacant as a winter pasture, to have smelled,
on the coldest day, the welcome warmth of urine and hay
from the just-opened barn door, returned
to the smell of coffee in the kitchen, fresh biscuit
and bacon, to have seen my wife's face slowly
brighten, her cheek regain its wild-rose blush
when I put my lips upon it, to have picked
and tasted the wild raspberry, sun-warmed,
sweet and sour as first dumb desire,
to have been partner with so much life,
to have lived this long, to have lived. . . .

General John Cabell Breckinridge
DECEMBER 31, 1862: THE MORNING OF
THE BATTLE

I wake before the sun, though
wake is wrong—I never really
slept, am still asleep, that line

between the two smudged out
by war's clumsy thumb.
My boots slip when I walk, suck

and stick, as if this earth, hungry,
strained to take me to its table.
No moon. I'm sure it's seen enough.

And yet, the sky eerily lit,
one star beneath the place, vacant,
where some moon should hang.

To save my life, I wear, on a cord
around my neck, an amulet from Jacob;
its faint aroma rises,

unfamiliar but pleasant.
At first, I said no, but he insisted—
I hope my God will understand.

Rain still falls, then freezes, as Frank,
our yellow mascot dog, joins me.
Hello, you scrawny loyal furry

bag of bones. No rabbits left
for you, old boy! Our hungry men
got every one, trap

even rats, fry them for breakfast.
They say the flesh is sweet—
but what it sweetened on. . . .

I hear the cattle, restless, slow,
starving now as well. Poor beasts
we breed to feed us! Their eyes grow round,

then rounder, as sharpened bones protrude.
One light across the river flickers
lit, a Federal beginning his breakfast

and Frank, licking my empty hand,
responsive as any dumb beast,
loyal even to our madness.

The sun will soon appear, orange.
How many left alive tonight
to watch it drop and set?

I did what I could. Reasoned, raged,
even wept before him —
but I was not enough.

Blue Ribbon Rosie (iii)

I was in the woods
with our neighbor's
son when it hit

    come to my arms
    you who are chipped
    who are splintered

he spoke to me
with his eyes
with his hands

    when ice melts
    it runs down
    any mountain

my babies slept
in their beds

    the sun's unfit
    for tenderness

    the cold moon
    casts no heat

my husband mended
the plow mare's harness
before the kitchen fire

    blood-red hooves will
    steal your life away

our cabin shattered
like an egg
dropped on frozen ground

    sorrow fills my eyes
    my throat   my mouth

I walked away from
what life I had
didn't turn around

    death who wears
    a wooden box
    refuses to let me in

General Breckinridge
TO GENERAL JUBAL EARLY
JUST BEFORE THE BATTLE

If I should die today,
let it be known I did

all in my power to save
these fated men, these boys.

Will Sommers, Confederate Soldier
Fix bayonets, prepare to attack. . . .

Hidden by darkness, we moved, no coffee,
cornmeal, or bacon to hush our complaining
bellies, the black sky's bitter rain
drumming our background melody.
Now we wait, feet and hands
numbing till we can barely stand.

Solid ground will soften, slop
for gallant fighting men to wallow in.
Nearly six . . . it seems a sin
to kill a sleeping man, drop
down on him, an armed angel —
don't sleep, this nightmare's moral!

Tired and alone, the first night at camp
in Tennessee, and not a one
of us could sleep. Tightly strung,
green as new-made banjos, we stamped
and clapped until one fool went moo
like a cow, and then another moo,

followed through the night by oinking pig,
barking dog, neighing horse, and dawn
brought in with human cock-crows and yawning
men who now must march and drill and dig.
What the night before had been a party,
became a never-ending penalty.

Then, that battle, our first, so strange,
began with loaded words thrown back
and forth, till someone shouted out, Jack,
that you, you low-down, stinking, mangy
dog? You could have served us sliced and fried,
it was Kentucky on the Union side!

Long beyond the order to attack,
we bullied, yelled, then all of us

CIVIL BLOOD

threw down our guns and loudly cussed,
grabbing, then socking, some Kentucky Jack.
And so it was we shouted, punched, and rolled,
ending our first major battle whole.

The worst of war is not the constant fear,
not the men who die, the bullets all
around. Instead, it is the days that follow
each and every battle: the moans, the tears,
the smells of everything that bullets left
behind, or rather, what they partially left. . . .

THE BATTLE

Tad Preston, Cadet
Fix bayonets, prepare to attack. . . .

Behind and just a little to my left,
Frank, the mascot dog, sits licking —
he's the only one who didn't laugh.
They called me baby boy; out loud I wept
to prove it. Called me blonde girl, picked
a winter bouquet of sticks, gave me half

and half to that crazy Rose who haunts our camp.
Father, I promise to fight like the honorable man
you'd have as son. Mother, I know I'll
never forget your face, your eyes, the lamp-
light blessing your words: Raise your hand
in anger, you said, against no living soul.

I have never been so scared, so cold.
My feet refuse to know my body, my hands
can barely button me up. Rain falls,
soaking my coat, then freezing. Now, I'm old,
Mother, old enough to raise a hand,
a gun, but out of fear, not anger. Tall

cedar trees around us darken the sky.
Last night, at dusk, our enemy's little band
across the river played Yankee Doodle,
and we sent back our Dixie in reply.
Then Hail Columbia to our grand
Bonnie Blue Flag. The homesick Federals,

caught in a foreign land, raised to the sky
our common song, Home Sweet Home.
I've never heard it played so sad.
Our band joined in, and, surprisingly, I,
away from home at Christmas and alone,
began to sing, I felt so moved, so bad.

CIVIL BLOOD

My voice—it sounded strange—rose far
above the trees. The men stilled, listening,
one by one began to sing, until, at the end,
our camps together in song, the night, dark,
had lightened. Nearby men, crying and laughing,
raised me to their shoulders, one of them.

John Cabell Breckinridge, General
Fix bayonets, prepare to attack. . . .

They raised him high upon their shoulders, a boy
that I must order in to fight our war.
I have one exactly that age. Our Owen
is just fourteen. And what will he store
up, remember, this boy? Hair so white—
he looked like a star above them, that bright,

and fragile—young, so young—too brave.
Under the cedar trees, surgeons sharpen
their knives and saws, gather up lint, save
it to dam the flood that will pool on rocks and
stumps. In red, your boots mark out a trail
of blood behind you, step by step, a wail.

I had four thousand sons when this war
began. Everything we know we lose. . . .
They joke: The surgeon, they say, opens his store
and waits for them to buy. They try to choose
their graves, wear name and next of kin pinned
upon their backs, try to stay free of sin—

before the battle at least, leave their cards
behind, carry a Bible, a favorite picture
of sweetheart, or wife and child. It's hard
to watch the magic they work to live, not sure
if anything will do. Men, boys,
God go with you, I had no choice. . . .

CIVIL BLOOD

Blue Ribbon Rosie (iv)

I went back once   saw
a stone foundation

captive of rain
prisoner of snow

what little the shells
left the fire had charred
black   and a chimney

our sorrow is naked
will not be clothed

dead they told me
all dead   hardly enough

to bury   but they put
up markers anyway

an empty alphabet
to imitate three lives

every night I hear
my babies crying

we who have fed
on the seed of war

fondle death
like a newborn

I run toward the cabin
but never get there

in time

Will Sommers, Confederate Soldier
Quiet now . . . attack!

wormy light, sky blue-black, elbow to elbow, silently we run,
all but one with loaded guns, ready to fire, reload and fire,
moving shadows melt from cedar brakes in single lines,
no sunrise red, wind an icy howl, two gray lines crouch,
move forward, no human sound but heave and suck of air
breathed out and in, running past whatever we've saved of our
childhoods, silent until we come upon them, then yelling, I
shoot from my empty gun round after round, while some, still
asleep are killed, curled in their canvas tents, some are
killed stirring their breakfast coals, some frying bacon
or making coffee, one sits holding his steaming cup, dead,
one, a fork and plate lifted slightly for some other meal
than the lead stuck in his opened belly, fear a final shadow
spread across his face, fear the drum behind this dance,
as men scramble for neatly stacked weapons, one is shot
pulling up suspenders, one just folding a woolen blanket,
two saying morning prayers, their Amens and Dear Lords
ending that familiar tune of faith once and for all,
and it's raining now, sky dumping more misery upon us,
as men fire one round, drop to reload, and I crouch,
then run and drop, faithfully going through these soldier
motions, once knocking over with my shoulder a Federal
sighted in on one of ours, flattening a tent around four
sleeping men, sky of fire and ash, stone struck against stone,
sparks lighting the white of an eye, the stump of an arm,
bone branching out, once flesh-covered, a scream, the hiss
of rain against fire, of fire against stone, of stone against
flesh, and all around me flesh is dying, and I, too, scream,
shout out all I have left of trust into the dark sky,
my own fear, its open mouth moving, carrying me across

Tad Preston, Cadet
Quiet now . . . attack!

over the hard ground toward the stream where a hundred
artillery horses tied halter to halter lower their big
heads to drink, and I must shoot them, every one, kill the
dapple gray, who goes down on one knee, kill the bay, who,
mouth open, rears, black mane and tail flying, sprays blood
from its mouth in a final red flag, kill the chestnut who
stands perfectly still, insides trailing out behind, such
surprise in that look, shoot the black who rears, whinnies,
turning once around like a dancer, tips back into the stream,
framed by foaming water, flying hooves and teeth and tails,
everything left alive screaming, everything dying, the dull
thunk after thunk of my bullets meeting solid flesh, and then,
I take one down, blonde as my hair, step across its back,
so broad I lose my balance, sit down on its side as it raises
a heavy head, looks up at me with brown eyes, more than human
in their trust, their questions I cannot answer, then one
breath heaved in and out, dies, this golden horse, gold of
wheat and summer sun, and just as I know there are angels,
I know the sky is daily stained with the cooled blood
of those who cannot speak for themselves

John Cabell Breckinridge, General
Quiet now . . . attack!

and I yell, On men! pushing them forward, when, without
warning, as drums beat out their long unbroken battle roll,
my newly captured horse, an elegant white, begins to step
in rhythm sideways, the whine of cannon ball, stops, slowly
turns around his outstretched leg, and though I rein him in,
has the bit between his teeth, shells exploding, black smoke,
begins to trot a small circle, head bobbing, then approaches
a stump, puts his front feet upon it, gracefully turning
around, the scream, the murmured prayer, as I, giving out
orders, turn a ludicrous circle, realize I've ridden a circus
horse into battle, his unyielding routine activated by drum
rolls, that relentless throb, and dismounting, I catch a
riderless bay, mount amidst clouds of powder smoke, yell
instructions, patch holes in the line, drums like hundreds
of pounding hearts, lift up behind me a wounded color bearer,
who, waving his flag, shouts over and over again, Here's your
Sixth Kentucky! his tattered, red-stained regimental flag
cut from Mary's wedding dress, death our only sacrament, men
cheering and shouting, know this round is theirs, hazy smoke
rising around us, red sun pulling itself up in the sky,
drums in my eyes, in my throat, in my chest, as far across
the field, scattered with blasted tents and hundreds of men
twisted like toy soldiers, faces contorted, I see my horse,
brilliantly white, trotting the sawdust of his own circus,
bullets hissing all around him, completing his flawless
performance to a background of dying and drums, unflinching

CIVIL BLOOD

Tad Preston, Cadet
Take the hill, men!

All together, we run uphill, cheering,
until the dark grove of evergreen
at the top lights up like Christmas.
Cannon! More of them than I can count!
They roll forward, fire down
on us. That roar nearly breaks my ears!
Our line stumbles, stops, advances
behind a single scrawny rabbit, flushed by
running feet, Frank barking just behind.
One Federal steps from somewhere,
laughing, sights in on Frank, my own
gun empty, no time, I scoop
a handful of rocks and mud,
step forward, aim and throw

Will Sommers, Soldier
Take the hill, men!

the mudball catches that soldier
directly in the center
of his forehead. Splat! I've never seen
a better shot! Frank bounds off,
barking, the Federal turns his gun. . . .
(Forgive me, I could have saved him.)
One shot, the boy goes down.
I roll him over. What a small
shape to carry so much death.
He still smiles.
Hearing that familiar hiss,
I look up, see, too late,
a cannon ball bouncing toward me, fall
aside as it wings me on the thigh

John Cabell Breckinridge, General
Take the hill, men!

he falls, they all are falling,
my men, without a nation,
state, or home. Without a chance.
I yell till I can shout
no more, trying, with my words,
to save them—slim defense
against a hill of cannon,
whose argument is death.
So this is war, the glory
we are bred and groomed for.
During the retreat, faces blackened,
they stumble past me. One says,
We were butchered, General!
I can only cry, My orphans, my poor orphans!

General Jubal Early
TO GENERAL BRECKINRIDGE
JUST AFTER THE BATTLE

What do you make
of States Rights
now, General?

CIVIL BLOOD

Blue Ribbon Rosie (v)

I built my house
on mud   I built
my dreams on man

    flesh of his flesh
    flesh of his flesh

the men in uniform
are as close to my loss
as I'm allowed

    you cannot reason
    with a cannon

blue ribbons tied in my hair
I dance for the soldiers
sing them battle songs

    say a prayer
    spin three times

    look in the sun
    in the eagle's eye

perhaps one of them
fired the cannon
that silenced my husband

stopped my babies' cries

    when flies buzz
    in your blood

    you can't leave death
    through a door

the weapons are stilled
for a sigh   for a name
called out in the night

you can't draw in
what fire has erased

the children took
my sorrow with them

I cannot weep
I cannot cry

madness is a song
the tune and words
cut away from the bone

flesh of my flesh
flesh of my flesh

WHAT REMAINS
III

Cabell's Escape Journal
MAY 6, 1865:
NEAR WASHINGTON, GEORGIA

Lee has surrendered. Federal troops approach
at a gallop, intent on arresting

President Davis and me;
they plan to hang us both.

I lead a small and tattered band, freakish
as a many-fingered glove. Pointing southeast
toward Florida, we hope to draw the troops

away from Davis, who still demands to fight —
temper outdistancing his judgment!

I send at a gallop a brief message to him:

It is folly to hold out
longer. We cannot squander
one more precious son.

· · ·

I've shaved my mustache, divided up my shirts,
collars hand-stitched artfully enough
by Mary to save my life. It hurt most

to give away my best tobacco and Kentucky bourbon.
Sainthood still escapes me —

I wept, but can't be sure just what the tears
were for — my broken South, my handmade shirts,
or losing such a fine mustache. . . .

I've saved my hunting jacket plus two
scant saddlebags of personal effects.

One letter from Mary warms a place
near my heart, and the last
scribbled words of Asa Lewis I promised
to give his mother after the war.

Jacob, who I have freed, will not
leave my side. Obstinate as ever,
he finally said, If I'm free, as you say,

I must be free enough to stay with you.

He's terrified of water. When I told him
we would cross the ocean, his eyes blinked,
but he would not budge.

. . .

Even his kind looks cannot light
the darkness of my thoughts.

I wonder what death awaits me,
prisoner of human skin,

offering up prayers to a deaf
sun, no map to guide me
from this world to the next.

THE SOUTH (I)

At the end, captured Federals die faster
than they can be counted.
You can smell the camp

three miles away, a church of death,
its baptism raging hunger,

communion cups, tins of watery soup,
haloes of black flies buzzing.

You can hear war's praises sung
by a choir raising their voices

to death; war's prayers, the gibberish
written into the talk of men
who saw more than words can bear.

When it finally ends, prisoners
released, many have faith
in nothing but starvation.

Cabell's Escape
MAY 20, 1865:
MILLWOOD PLANTATION

Dear Mary, Our world
disintegrates — chunks
of land float free,
figures drop off
despite black line. . . .
Col. Dickison, old
Swamp Fox, shapes our
escape Atlantic coastward
along St. John's River
until we give in to the sea.
Remember memory's five
childish fingers ticking
off Atlantic, Pacific,
Indian, Arctic, Antarctic?
Salted pale blue, our
globe spun, more water
than land. The borders
of my days obscured by
squalls and fickle sun,
my spirits wax and wane.
And this oppressive heat!
Airborne, the sweet bloom
of huckleberry weakens our
defenses until, bound
and gagged, stagnant
water revolts us.
Our days, disproportionate,
run over with boredom
or danger's frothy brew.
We long for night's
unconscious release, find
sleep a golden line
heavy hung with nightmare.
Mary, I see it clearly now:
honor, our double reins,
tradition, our tied knot —

our love not large enough,
our fear greater than
whatever it would take
to break another trail
toward a form of freedom
we couldn't comprehend,
much less imagine.
They would hang me,
stripped of my little honor,
as one might murder
reflections fractured
by water, the soft
ravel of fabric. . . .
What survives remains
yours alone, John

CIVIL BLOOD

THE SOUTH (II)

When wind tips up the blackbird,
ruffles the red of his wing, tumbles

poplar leaves from silver to green,
we tremble between two worlds, as

the spirits of slaughtered horses return.

We who have raised you from colts,
ridden you, sleek and full-muscled,
into the cannon's mouth

live on, half man, half death,
wait for the drum roll of hooves,

the spirits of slaughtered horses returning.

Herds of dark shadows, they flee the smoldering
cities of men, smoke rising
into skies turned against the earth.

Those who could carry us over
have gone on before.

The spirits of slaughtered horses return,

their eyes red as our final sun,
their hooves flailing our shallow graves.
Fierce dogs whine and shiver.

Only the mules survived, running
at the guns' first warning coughs,
but the horses obeyed, stood like statues

to receive the guns' final words.

After each battle, bellies of dead horses
swelled into mountains across a flattened field.

The meadow lies hushed, remembering.

Children chase each other in circles,
roll in grass grown over the shrapnel,

as if there is no history, as if our lives
are not a play on forgetting.

The spirits of slaughtered horses return. . . .

CIVIL BLOOD

Cabell's Escape Journal
MAY 25, 1865: FLORIDA

Pruned to bare limb by the heat. We fall ill.
Weaken daily. Our zone of loss enlarges. Waiting

for Col. Dickison to raise a sunken boat for us,
we rested first at Millers, then Sumner's Wauchula.

Davis was captured almost at once.

Some song plays itself over and over. In my head.
I cannot name or even hum it, though I have often tried.
Vegetation here grows lush, thick as a jungle.

It frightens me. The intensity of green.

Even flowers are carnivorous, eat the insects feeding
on our flesh. Hunting for deer, I sat upon a log.
Waiting. When our dogs delivered a stag,

we put an end to its terror.

Escape feels more like punishment than freedom.

What I once called principle or truth
I now regard utility — the greed required

to feed our own desires. I cannot look
at my face in the mirror —

a boy returns my stare. Those eyes, open wide,
shimmer in the flames consuming the field.
Muskets explode. Screams. Then smoke.

Where, I wonder, does forgiveness reside?

Sitting on that log, red ticks bit me. Fore
and aft. I scratched my ankles, my other
parts raw — they blister and ooze. Nature

provides me conscience. I pay all night penance.
Itching. Burning. This flesh a heavy load.
And lost.

THE SOUTH (III)

A woman uses up her last
two potatoes for soup.
The onion is wrinkled,

crackles like paper when
she chops it, yet the soup
smells better for it.

From her kitchen window,
she sees two black crows
perched on the split-rail fence.

She wishes for a carrot,
one sliced carrot, to float up,
orange, in so much white.

Cabell's Escape Journal
JUNE 3, 1865:
INDIAN RIVER, ATLANTIC COAST

When morning dawns, though overcast, it's some relief
from last night's constant roar —

storming all around us in the dark,
bull alligators,
                huge tails thrashing water

into foam from their bloody
mating rage, passion fueled by a brainless

wisdom that burns in the craw,
the chest, at the base of the spine,

passion that nothing will quench,

even at dawn when I pump bullet
after bullet into the big one floating close by,

as he opens his jaws, issues that quavering hiss.
Inside the jaws, that flesh

is colored almost human.
                As I fire again,

he bellows, roaring, tail propelling him toward
our flimsy boat, that gutteral sound, his musky smell,

those yellow, unfeeling eyes.

I fire again, again, until his jaws slowly
close, and, hissing, he spins in slowing

spirals, churned water foaming red,
as I pump three more shots into

that head where some brain should be. Spellbound,
I can't stop firing,

shoot out both the eyes, can't stop firing.

Then Jacob pulls me down beside him, strokes
my forehead, softly murmurs, as one might speak

to a child awakened by nightmare.

There, there, Master, he says,
everything's fine now,

everything's fine. . . .

THE SOUTH (IV)

The war, they say, is over.
Slave no longer,
the old carpenter, hands knotted,
is no less hungry.
When the scavengers rode off
with his daughter,
he heard her screaming his name
long after it
was silent. Then he got
a gun and bullets,
and, with that gun, he shot
a rabbit, but found
no wood to cook it over.
War has eaten
every tree for miles around.
Muscle and bone,
his rabbit demands some
serious cooking.
He must chop up the birdhouse
that, years ago,
he built for his wife's wrens,
even the pole,
and as fire turns the rabbit
in the pot toward
tenderness, from the throat
of flame, he hears
the warbling song that seasoned
his May mornings.

Cabell's Escape
JUNE 6, 1865:
INDIAN RIVER, ATLANTIC COAST

My Dearest Mary, Evening. The sun sinks, spitting
angry fire. This, my last letter before attempting
the Gulf Stream.

Our craft, three men in length, holds six. Sunk
to the gunwales. One sail, a rope, hand-held, four
oars. It seems a fragile thing to sail the ocean in.

The Gulf Stream capricious, choppy.
The trough between waves widens.

Jacob, terrified beyond words, sits at my feet
clutching my knees. His silence is wrenching.

St. John's River spun us in circles. Flowing
supposedly north. But sinuous, deceitful. Our compass
touched one direction, then another.

Channel after channel—darkened by moss-hung
palm, slash pine, cypress—turned out to be dead-end.

On the banks, pelican, crane. Small deer
watched us with their round eyes.

Every night, an inquisition of mosquitoes; they target us
the way bullets found the Zouaves' red jackets.
Permit no negotiation.

We slap with both hands. Wrap up in the sail. Nothing
shields us. Some nights, we bury ourselves in sand,
then worry about snakes gliding across our faces.

That first night, loaded down with two weeks' supplies,
we anchored, mid-stream, in torrential rain. Nearly

sank. Tried to sleep, soaked, sitting upright.
Our gunpowder ruined, most of the food. Next day, we dined
on wet cornmeal. Rum and water. No one spoke as we ate.

We happened on an orchard, deserted but for hundreds
of lemons — every tree stooped over in abundance.

Acres of brilliant suns beaming. We made lemonade
from their juice, a bit of dirty sugar. A squalid
treat. Richer in anticipation than taste.

This encyclopedia of trees! I saw a Manchinell —
so poisonous, to even stand beneath its branches, receive
its morning dew, proves fatal. Sea grape, pond apple,

strangler fig, first depriving its host of sun.
Then life. Geigers bloom, their orange and crimson
trumpets swinging in constant summer breeze.

The peace here feels fatal.
I think trees speak through the air all night.

We glided past a camp of Federals, faces eerily under-
lit by blazing fire. We raised our oars, used the river's
course as our escape. Then laughed until we nearly
capsized. We could not stop ourselves.

Alligators slip by like gunboats, half submerged. Black
scales slicing the water's surface.

Thirty miles we portaged overland, boat sliding off
the oxen-hauled cart. Later, swollen, mutilated
by black flies, the beasts had to be put away.

Between mosquitoes and black flies, a man,
hands tied, would be drained dry in a day.

We fear, constantly, brain fever. No antidote
but slapping. Those who curse find some relief.
Momentarily.

Hundreds of dead eyes—their constant stare.

I can't conjure a reason for my life upon this earth.

Our boat tips forward and back, forward and back
between this life and the next.

Death's all that's given to end this life.
But memory can't be killed. It rises
like flames in a dry field.

You can't return to what you were.

The sun! Brilliance illuminating nothing.
Objects flatten out against natural backdrops. Color
stripped of intensity by intensity even greater.

My grasp on this world weakens. The next could not
be worse. Yours beyond any outcome, John

THE SOUTH (V)

Through one night, the entire next day,
in an emptied parlor, oak floor
running red with blood,

three surgeons bend over three
separate tables, curse and sweat,

throw sawed-off limbs out the open windows.

No one free to mop, no morphia
or chloroform to mask the pain.

When the soldier comes to, his right
arm's gone, stump bandaged.

Years later, before his eyes,
open or closed, piles of autumn leaves
become a tangle of bloody arms.

All the arms are right arms.

He gets home, hauled like an empty sack
on the back of a farmer's wagon.
The stump, infected, sends the infection
through him, has its way with him.

He doesn't know his wife or son,

thinks they're trying to kill him.
The farmer helps them tie him
on the bed, legs spread and strapped still,

arm tied to the headboard, clenched fist
banging it over and over again,
his wife whispering through her sobs,
I'm sorry, James, I'm sorry.

Now he sits on the bed,
better, but engulfed in a darkness
of cloud refusing to rain or pass over.

The farmer next door has plowed
the back field for seeding,

cursing his ancient horse up and down
the furrows choked with weeds,
part of his endless war
on what grows but doesn't nourish.

Through the open door, sunshine.
Far off, beyond the apple tree,
brilliant in white blossom,
he sees his wife and boy

setting the tobacco, carrying the plants
from the bed by the side of the house.

She has scattered the seed.
But who will plow the corn? And then
there's the hay to cut before

reaping the little crop of wheat.
He feels, at once, needed and
discarded like a worn-out winter coat.

A pair of cardinals glide in to peck
at crumbs close to the pig trough.

The female leads the way; the male
follows, timid at first, then
struts out in his red suit.

They peck and eat, then touch beaks,
touch and eat again.

The man walks to the door,
stands in the morning light.

Sighing, giving in to the seasons,
the earth's hunger, he picks up a bag

of manure, slings the rope handle
over his shoulder above the healed stump.
The woman and boy see but say nothing,

as he begins, one handful at a time,
feeding the hidden new seed.

CIVIL BLOOD

Cabell's Escape Journal
JUNE 9, 1865:
BY FORT DODGE, FLORIDA

O'Toole works his magic mouth, returns, canoe loaded
with food. We pass it around. Name it
as if saying our first words:

ham, oranges, flour, salt pork—and water, fresh water!

Delmonico's never served better! As we eat, more savage
than civil, a flock of flamingoes, all necks and legs,

flies over, as unreal in their pink against blue
as our bodies crouched against sand, the relentless sun.

At midnight, we push off, overloaded with food. Muddled
as ever, Wilson, acting as helmsman, nearly sinks us.

Trapped between shallow reefs, Wood takes the rudder.

Throwing our ham, oranges, and flour overboard,
we're silent as farmers forced to burn their barns.

I sink into despair. Then Jacob shows me
what he's hidden under the folded sail.

My best Kentucky bourbon! The only medicine
that can unfurl my spirits—but not a lasting remedy.

All night we wander through a maze of ocean paths
heading for the open mouth of sea, hunger twisting
our stomachs, the memory of ever being full
washed away.

. . .

Jacob's grown silent since he discovered
I plan to sail for Europe from Cuba—

providing we reach Cuba. . . .

He can't abide the sea. Though he hates
deserting me, he wants the freedom

promised him. I fear for what
he'll find back home,
but have agreed to send him,

along with a letter praising
his loyalty so he can find work.

His absence will make a hole in my life,
but I'll say nothing to change his mind.

Any freedom he can find is due him.

He watches me, convinced I can't
survive without him. His eyes hold
so much love. Such sadness.

· · ·

Rain doesn't measure itself drop by drop,
and the ocean feels no remorse for its raging.

The tree cannot remember its yearly loss
of leaves, foresee spring's regenerative green.
One raindrop reflects the sun, the moon,

the stars, the entire curve of this earth,
but there's no recognition in what
returns my stare. Below, fish collect

rainbow colors, scatter the spectrum like coins
across a polished floor. This prayer:

forgiveness for injury, grace
against despair.

CIVIL BLOOD

THE SOUTH (VI)

Though the air is seductive with lily
and hyacinth, even spring cannot

reproduce the gracious house burned down
to foundation beside this garden. Lush,
beyond the scope of bullets' range,

here the redbud, brushed pink over branches'
black line, shouts out like a celebration.
Protected by twin lions, each stone, epistle

of faith in order's rule, the formal
garden blooms. Pears sleep in the orchard
under white blossoms, the canary singing
them slowly awake. The hour before

dawn is stillest, birds rising as always
to fly around that space once occupied
by a house. Three sons returned,

one by one, to rest nearby. You can almost
hear them laughing in the emptiness
their rooms no longer fill. A gold-framed

mirror where they surveyed their first
grown-up suits is gone. Gone, too,
the blue and red bottles, soft morning

light humming through them,
and the petitpoint footstool, ten years
of color sewn into its rose design.

Bees burrow into feasts of blossom,
shimmering dew bends grass over
dreams of deer passed by in the night

leaving behind divided footprints
of remembrance. If the peacocks returned,
their cries would sound alarm,
one bird trailing the brilliance of greens

and blues above the ground where,
hastily wrapped in gray cloth and buried,

rests the family silver. It will not
be stolen now. The silver platter
holds its dark portion of abundance,

the silver tea service has grown cold
waiting, and in the open sugar bowl,
curled in a circle, a single earthworm.

EXILE AND FREEDMAN
IV

Cabell
JUNE 11, 1865:
CROSSING THE GULF STREAM
TO CUBA

Midnight. We're cast into the sea.
Our moon, risen full and orange,

throws a river of light across
deep water. Six figures crouch,
dark shadows across water's

solemn, moon-slick surface.
Our small boat follows a single lantern
into night mist. Rowing across the moon's

orange river, our boat, its hunched
inhabitants, blaze with light. Somewhere,

on the other side of darkness,
our sun burns upon itself, violence
lighting orange our moon, our way.

* * *

All night, we move steadily ahead,
then, becalmed, bake like slabs of fish
in scorching sun, our small band

decomposing into anger, whine, and plea.
As if in penance for past speech,
our tongues swell to fill our mouths.

Jugs of water empty, turtle eggs gone bad,
we pray for rain. We pray.

The sea holds us captive, steals
our meager supply of strength,
feeds us despair.

That night, the prayed-for rain arrives,
and wind spawning waves rearing
fifteen feet above us.

We cannot sail. We cannot steer. Just bob
about between one nightmare, crested white,

and then another. Holding on the only action
left us, all night we toss and roll,

swallowing salty water with each sputtering
breath, till life itself
is punishment enough.

                    . . .

Finally I sleep, too sick to sit upright.
Delirious, I see our river at the Dale, see

my father's face, the portrait face, but now,
alive! and in his look, such love.

He speaks, but I cannot make out the words,
nothing but the love in them,

until his face blurs, drops,
and, rising from the river, an alligator.
He must be twenty feet in length!

His blunt snout noses toward me,
jaws slowly open, flesh

inside them pale as my thigh,
and hissing a warning,

comes at me, exposed throat dark
as the hunger inside him,

for he would pull me from the boat,
roll me under the waves,

but I shout, No!
wake in Jacob's arms; open my eyes

to see the storm passed, the wind
a docile breeze. Jacob has not slept.

To cradle me, he sat bolt upright
through the night, as terrified
as any man alive.

Suddenly, he points!

Ahead in the dark, a lighthouse beam.
Land, sweet land! and bells
and thanks and bells! Red and gold,

the sun rises on Cuba and our freedom.

We see a dock, chickens in crates,
and coconuts. Then people!

Waving, they run to welcome us,
shout words we cannot understand.

Jacob
NOVEMBER 1866:
THE YEAR OF JUBILEE

I've had enough of any ocean.
Coming home to find my freedom,
got so sick on the boat,

could hardly lift my head.
An old gray tomcat nobody
wanted gave me some comfort.

I named him Moon 'cause he had just
one eye. Back on Southern land,

I gave my feet their freedom, went to
where I've never been. Carried Moon
in a bundle on my back.

When I'd call, Here Moon, he'd
cry out his cracked meow.

Freedmen killed all along the road
for walking their freedom. One day,
I saw five dead all different ways.

Saw a boy about fifteen hung
from a tree. Pinned to his shirt,

a sign: Beware Nigger!
This Tree Wants Your Neck Too!

In every Southern town, freedmen
march in parades. Bands,
lots of soldiers, preachers

walk with their Bibles open,
women dressed in white,
and little children, singing.

Then people march with tools
they plan to use now they're free,

and two broke-down horses pull
a wagon with a slave block
covered black as death.

The women watching cry out,
Give me back my children!

I ask everywhere, but can't find
Manda, know for sure that Sam

is dead. I settle in Kentucky,
outside Paris, to work for
Mr. King, help him harvest

his tobacco. He lets me plow
a little land, grow some collard
greens, okra, yellow squash.

I keep five hens, all white,
a rooster, and one pig
I hope to fatten up.

Save for my farm—but slow.
Had to sign a piece of paper

saying I won't get paid till
year's end when crops are in.

After sundown, I teach night school
in my shack; freedmen come from
miles around. I don't know much,

but can read and write,
teach them what I know.

Cabell

FEBRUARY 1869:
THE LONG WAY HOME

In the past, I often wished for time,
and now that I've nothing

but time, minute by minute,
I wish it away.

Mary and I stay at the Grand Hotel
in Paris. Many expatriates live here.
(Ten thousand of us wander Europe,

searching for a second home.)
My income in a state of disaster,
I tutor other exiles' children.

Our son, Cabell, beyond anyone's help,
wanders across the conquered South.
Friends say he can't keep a job,

seems confused but sober—
some consolation.

So far removed, I can do little
to help him but worry. Day after day,
I damn this fruitless life of exile.

Those still in Kentucky urge my return—
impossible until I'm granted
full pardon by President Johnson.

I miss little Mary, studying in New York,
write her every day. Send stamps
to Clifton, set upon a law career,

explain to him how much
in the world demands doing,
suggest he consider Engineering,

a profession where he might build
something lasting, make a profit,
be of use.

. . .

I came the long way home, traveled
to pass the time. This large world
is darker than I imagined.

In Athens, I stood on the hill where
Pericles addressed the assembled citizens.

Spent a long hour in Socrates' prison,
imagining how it must feel
to accomplish your own death.

Convinced the South made a terrible
mistake from which it may never recover,

I keep thinking of other courses
we might have followed.

I crossed the Germanies, and, in Italy,
came across, suddenly, an American ship
resting at anchor in the harbor.

The sight of its flag, flying proudly,
wrenched my heart. I knew we must return
to our native soil, and Mary agreed.

. . .

Six months after returning to Canada
and renting a cottage where we can see
our homeland from nearly every window,

on Christmas day, I'm fully pardoned.

Not wanting to appear too eager, we wait
until February to return. Hand in hand,

Mary and I cross the suspension bridge
over the Niagara to set foot on native soil.

Then, travel back to our beloved Bluegrass.

Sunset, storm clouds gathering.
When the train hisses into Lexington,
a huge downpour is in progress.

Those assembled are not daunted,
somehow keep their bonfires burning.
As I step onto the train platform,

they cheer, play soggy but spirited
versions of Dixie, Home Sweet Home,
Hail To The Chief. A final cheer,

and someone cries, Down umbrellas!
They fold their umbrellas in unison,

then stand, silent and drenched,
waiting for me to speak.

Jacob
FEBRUARY 1869:
FREEDOM'S LYNCHING

Uncle Sam promised us forty acres,
gave us Kukluxers; promised us
a mule, gave us a lynching.

Uncle Sam broke every promise he made.

The Kukluxers have me on their list.
First, they shot up the night school,

threw fire balls in the windows,
burned our reader.

Scholars too afraid now to come.

Once I decided to vote, things
got even worse. Came home one night,

my white hens were hanging
from the sugar maple,

the rooster cut up in pieces
on the floor of my shack,

windows smeared red
with chicken blood.

When I found Mr. King, asked him
to tell the Freedmen's Bureau,

he looked at his feet. Scared.
So I went myself,

told them I'd talk in court
too, if they'd let me.

Kukluxers kill us, one by one,
any freedman who reads or preaches.

Those white men want us dead or gone.

Master sends money, a letter
telling where he's been.

When I read it, he seems so far,
I lean against the sugar maple,

stay there a long time,
my face in my hands.

Cabell
MARCH 1870: LAST BATTLES

I make a modest living
from law, the railroad, and our new
preoccupation, life insurance,

though we Southerners can't pay
for our lives, much less,
our deaths. Jacob works for us,

helps with handy work.
His property's been destroyed
by men still at war—

but now, with former slaves.
I give him what help I can.

Freedmen are disarmed, then beaten.
I hear stories of such wanton cruelty,
I'm ashamed my skin is white.

Ignoring the advice of family
and friends, I've taken a public stand

against the Klan, called them
bandits, idiots, and villains.

Strong words. Mary fears for my life.

There have been threats, but if
they'll resort to violence. . . .

Although the thought of arguing
the prosecution is abhorrent to me,

I've announced I'll prosecute
anyone harassing a freedman.

Whether I agree or not, the freedman's
constitutional right to vote,

even to testify against a white,
must be upheld.

This barbaric slaughter must end.

Although I've cautioned Jacob not
to anger the Klan, he insists
on exercising his freedom. I understand,
but I can do so little to protect him,
can only pray my name will keep him alive.

I refuse to speak at any Confederate
celebration or war memorial. It's time
we look toward the future.

. . .

After my statement to the press,
calling old friends bandits,

my stomach roils. I ride out
to the Dale, no longer family land

except in memory. The Indian mounds
rise above the Elkhorn River,

now swollen with spring rain.
Sycamores line the river banks,
scarred trunks gleaming white.

Mares frisk about, aware, perhaps,
that breeding season's about to begin.
In one pasture, an old trotter

enjoys his retirement. I can't imagine
a conscience as clear as his.

He stops eating, plods over to me,
his once fine legs swollen
at the knee joints. We survey

each other for some time. I note
the gray on his muzzle, his sway back.

He looks at my gray hair,
my ample stomach, but we remember
our breeding, say nothing.

I pat his face. He nuzzles my hand,
resumes grazing as I ride away.

Jacob
MARCH 1870: LAST BATTLES

After midnight, the Kukluxers ride
up again, so many,
I can't count them all.

My bare hands are not worth much
against their shotguns.

They rip the chimney off my shack,
then the roof. Say to me, You file

a complaint? We'll give you something
to complain about. Strip me, beat
me till I don't know my name.

Sheets can't cover, and I know
two of them by their fancy boots:

the white teacher from Frankfort,
and one circuit court judge
who just got on.

• • •

I move to Lexington, work for
Mr. Stuart in his store.
As a boss, he's not so good,

still hurts from a hip wound
outside Atlanta. Even though

he's always reading the Bible,
nothing makes him smile.
I do my best, work even Sunday,

late, sweep and take trash out,
sleep in the shed between nails
and bags of flour,

read by candlelight. Some nights
I learn about so many things,
just want to rip the book apart.

Work for Master Cabell too.
He helps me out. Kukluxers stole
the little I had saved.

Master's looking poorly. I pray
for his good health, tell him

to eat and sleep right—
but he never does.

. . .

I'm going to vote in August,
and in November too.

If those Kukluxers come again,
they'll have to kill me

to stop my vote.

Am kept company by that old
Moon cat. He was some trouble
to travel with. Complained

every step of the way, like I did
on the boat. He's so scared

of Kukluxers, hears a horse,
and hides behind a bag of flour.

But my old bones are tired
of hiding, need to stand

straight up. I have repented
for my sins, pray I'll meet Manda,
Grampa Sam, and Marcie up in heaven

where we'll shine out gold
like angels, moving free.

I had a dream where God
gives me paint, a brush,
and wings, so I begin

to paint. It calms my mind.
I draw birds on dry wood.
Use house paint from the store.

The bird that God sends flies up
in my mind and I catch it best I can.

First, a meadow lark — the yellow
and stripes are stubborn
to set down on the wood.

Then I paint a crow, try to coax
the blue out of the black,

and all the while I paint, I sing.

NOTES

The People:

An explanation of my word choice to describe black Americans: Although the term, *black*, was not widely accepted and used until the Civil Rights era of the 1960s, because of the political considerations of language and the demands of my own historical period, I have often chosen to use it in this book.

I. CABELL AND JACOB

Cabell: "Portraits of the Fathers. . . " — p. 18

The only way young Cabell knew either his father or grandfather was from portraits by Matthew Jouett and others that hung at Cabell's Dale. At the time of Cabell's grandfather's death at forty-six, probably from tuberculosis, John Breckinridge was Thomas Jefferson's Attorney General. He was also one of the largest slaveholders in Kentucky, owning fifty-seven slaves. Cabell's father died at the age of thirty-five, probably from a virulent strain of influenza. At the time of his death, he had served three terms in the Kentucky House of Representatives, and was serving a term as Secretary of State.

Cabell was influenced more by his grandfather—Jefferson's generation—than by his father or his father's generation. Although Cabell never owned more than five slaves himself, he was against slavery in principle but not in fact.

The river referred to in this poem is actually known as the Elkhorn Creek. Here and elsewhere, I have altered fact when dictated by poetic sense or sound.

As little boys, slaves were issued large shirts of homespun fabric. They weren't given long pants until they began to work in the fields at thirteen or fourteen. If they had grown quickly, their shirts by that time were indecently short.

Cabell: "Laetitia, Little Sister" — p.19

Cabell's mother never regained her emotional stability after his father's untimely death. So much tension existed between Cabell's mother and Laetitia that, at one time, an uncle suggested the girl be taken away from her.

Cabell: "The Reasons I Cry" — p. 21

Cabell, raised by women embroiled in emotional strife, was a very sensitive child. Although he mastered his emotions somewhat in later years, he always cried easily, a tremendous burden to him.

Jacob: "How I Learn . . . (i)" — p. 22

Kentucky law did not prohibit teaching slaves to read, but it was definitely discouraged.

"Patterroller" was one of the slave words for the night patrols.

Slaves were often expected to attend the Master's church on Sunday to hear a specially selected preacher preach on the blessings of obedience. Some all-black churches existed as well, especially in larger cities like Louisville. However, on week nights slaves often had their own prayer meetings with their own preachers. Because slave owners feared insurrection, slaves were often prohibited from meeting in groups. For this reason, prayer meetings were held secretly.

Cabell: "My Grandmother Black Cap" — p. 28

Although expecting to join her dead husband any moment, Grandmother Black Cap outlived him by fifty-two years.

Cabell: "Moving From Virginia to Kentucky. . . " — p. 30

After land in Virginia was depleted, Cabell's grandparents and their four children — one of them Cabell's father — moved to Kentucky. First, however, they sent the slaves ahead to break the land and build the house.

It took few slaves to run a farm (as they were called in Kentucky). Thus, the majority of the slave force was used as rental property. Slaves were contracted out for a certain period of time; then, they were sent off to work in new clothing. At the end of the contract, they were expected to be returned in new clothing as well. During the contract period, they were often allowed to return home only once a year, over the Christmas holidays, for a week to see their families.

Cabell: "What Grandmother Black Cap Told Me. . . " — p. 32

Of the four children, only Cabell's father survived the first year in Kentucky.

Cabell: "With Laetitia at the Indian Mounds. . . " — p. 39

On a rise overlooking the Elkhorn, in the thick forest of the estate, the children found ancient Adena Indian mounds where they often played.

Jacob: "How I Learn. . . (iv)" — p. 40

At the time of his death, John Breckinridge owned some of the finest livestock in the state. It's estimated that his herd of racing Thoroughbreds consisted of over two hundred mares, fillies, and colts.

Jacob: "Moving to the Big House" — p. 41

Slaves' life expectancies significantly increased if they were house slaves rather than field slaves. Because Jacob's father was white, and Jacob was a lighter color, he could also suffer from the dislike of darker slaves. His color, however, gave him a better chance of serving in the house. Young slaves were often "auditioned" to see if they were entertaining enough to be a "playboy" or "playgirl"—in other words, a babysitter. From this time on, Jacob took care of Cabell and Laetitia.

Jacob: "What Grampa Sam Told Me. . . "—p. 43

"Just came off the boat," was a phrase used by blacks to describe a very dark slave recently arrived from Africa.

Jacob: "How I Learn. . . (v)"—p. 46

A " 'broad" husband was one who lived abroad—on some other estate owned by another Master. If the couple were lucky, they saw each other once or twice a week, unless they risked the night patrols and visited at night without a pass.

Slaves dreaded to be sold "down river" to states like Louisiana, because the death rate was so high in those states.

Cabell: "At Eleven, I Write to Laetitia. . . "—p. 52

When he was ten years old, Cabell was sent away to school—years he remembered as the happiest of his childhood.

Cabell: "Journal Entries. . . "—p. 64

Cabell abhorred violence. It is interesting to note that, as a lawyer, he would only argue the defense.

Cabell: "The Wedding"—p. 69

Thanks to William Carlos Williams, and his poem, "The Dance," for this form.

Cabell: "Running For State Representative. . . "—p. 71

Cabell was just twenty-eight when elected to the Kentucky House of Representatives.

Cabell: "Memories of my Southern Education. . . "—p. 82

English law, the basis of American law, did not recognize slavery. Thus, the slave in America had no protection as a human being under law—legally, the slave was invisible.

II. THE BATTLE

"Introducing General Braxton Bragg. . . "—p. 113

Bragg and other Civil War generals fought the Civil War as they had fought the Mexican War. They were still wedded to frontal attack even after the rifled musket, easily reloaded, made frontal attack a study in mass murder.

"Will Sommers, Confederate Soldier, Speaks . . . "—p. 134

The final seven lines of "The Last Words of Asa Lewis" (from "Comrades . . . Good-bye") are those he actually uttered; they were too eloquent as delivered to alter. This speech is reproduced in the description of the execution in *Johnny Green of the Orphan Brigade: The Journal of a Confederate Soldier*, edited by Albert D. Kirwan, Lexington, Kentucky, 1959, on pages 59–61. Cabell kept Lewis's possessions for the duration of the war, and then, through his escape and exile. After returning to the United States, he delivered them to Lewis's mother, as promised.

Tad Preston, Cadet: "Fix Bayonets. . . "—p. 150

Cabell fought at Shiloh, Chickamauga, Chatanooga, New Market, and Cold Harbor, as well as at Murfreesboro or Stones River. These poems and the battle poems that follow take many incidents of the war and telescope them into one battle. Actually, it was later in the war, at the battle of New Market in May of 1864, that Breckinridge conscripted boys, fourteen to sixteen years old, from the Virginia Military Academy.

Tad Preston, Cadet: "Quiet Now . . . Attack"—p. 155

During the war, artillery horses were often slaughtered to halt the other side's movement of cannon.

John Cabell Breckinridge, General: "Quiet now. . . "—p. 156

Many Kentucky volunteers from the Bluegrass region furnished their own horses, often riding excellent Saddlebreds descended from Gaines' Denmark (f. 1851). This breed was known for its endurance, beauty, and courage. During the war, Kentucky lost about 90,000 horses and 37,000 mules. When horses were killed, volunteers rode whatever mounts they could find. For more information about Kentucky horses, see *The Horse World of the Bluegrass*, by Mary E. Wharton and Edward L. Bowen, edited by Bruce Denbo, published by The John Bradford Press, Lexington, Kentucky, 1980.

III. WHAT REMAINS

"Cabell's Escape: June 6, 1865 . . . "—p. 177

The Zouaves, patterned after the French Algerian army corps, were expertly trained New York and Pennsylvania forces of marching and fighting volunteers. They wore red pantaloons, white turbans, and blue and scarlet uniforms. Even after they suffered high casualties, they only reluctantly changed their uniforms to duller hues.

IV. EXILE AND FREEDMAN

Jacob: "November 1866: The Year of Jubilee"—p. 191

The account of this parade is from an article in the New York *Daily Tribune*, April 4, 1865. Parades were held all across the South that summer after the war ended, according to *The Trouble They Seen: Black People Tell the Story of Reconstruction*, edited by Dorothy Sterling, published by Doubleday & Company, Inc., Garden City, New York, 1976.

Sharecropping—a system where laborers work on credit—began in the South very soon after the war, often because landowners had no cash until crops were harvested. The system not only kept laborers in debt, but kept them tied to land they didn't own.

Cabell: "February 1869: The Long Way Home"—p. 194

Cabell feared he would be imprisoned or hanged if he returned home. As an exile and a symbol of the defeated South, he believed that he should be pardoned and granted full rights as an American citizen.

William C. Davis's excellent book, *Breckinridge: Statesman, Soldier, Symbol*, by Louisiana State University Press, Baton Rouge, Louisiana, 1974, contains a thorough account of Breckinridge's years of exile.

Jacob: "February 1869: Freedom's Lynching"—p. 197

The slogan, "Forty acres and a mule," referred to the need for freedmen to be given some means of livelihood after years of slavery. The Southern Homestead Act, passed by Congress and signed by President Johnson on June 21, 1866, set aside forty-five million acres of public land in five Southern states for freedmen to homestead. Designated to be no larger than eighty acres, the plots were free except for a five-dollar registration fee. However, much of the land was inferior, and few former slaves had enough money to buy the livestock and implements necessary to equip a successful farm. Of those few who did get started farming, most were run off or killed when their farms' former owners were pardoned and returned to the South. Although Kentucky was not one of the five states included under the act, most freedmen knew about it and felt they were entitled to some portion of the land they had worked on as slaves for so many years.

A group of white men in Kentucky, who originally called themselves the "Regulators," later made up the Ku Klux Klan. Their violence against blacks was not only meant to replace former slave codes, but to drive blacks from the South altogether. For a short period of time, rural blacks were killed or chased off their farms because many white Southerners hoped to import Chinese and Italian laborers to replace blacks. When this plan failed, blacks were, once again, welcomed back to labor on the land.

The Civil Rights Act, passed over President Johnson's veto in April 1866, guaranteed freedmen full civil rights. By 1866, all of the secession states and border states except Kentucky had granted blacks civil rights, including the controversial right to testify against whites in court. However, not until April 1872, was Kentucky forced to begin admitting black testimony in court. For a detailed account of this six-year legal battle, see Victor B. Howard's *Black Liberation in Kentucky: Emancipation and Freedom, 1862-1884*, the University Press of Kentucky, 1983.

Before the Fifteenth Amendment was ratified in March 1870, blacks organized a Negro Republican Party and prepared themselves to vote. According to Victor B. Howard, when the Colored Men's State Convention met in February in Louisville, nearly a hundred counties were represented.

Because of the destruction of the hope for full black political, economic, and social equality after the war, historians often refer to the Reconstruction period as the nadir of black history in America.

Cabell: "March 1870: Last Battles" — p. 199

Cabell's Dale is now part of the Castleton Farm, known for its excellent Standardbred horses.

William C. Davis states that Klan activity in Kentucky was severely curtailed by Breckinridge's public stand against it.

ACKNOWLEDGEMENTS

A project stretching over eight years owes a large debt for aid in its birth to the people who supported it. I'd like to express my gratitude to John W. Fenn; my five children; the Bush Foundation for a generous fellowship; the Minnesota State Arts Board for two grants; Alice Ryerson, and the Ragdale Foundation, Lake Forest, Illinois, for indispensable aid in writing time; Lisel Mueller; Marisha Chamberlain; James Moore; Chad Breckenridge and Sally Brown; Deborah Keenan; Patricia Hampl; Phebe Hanson; Mahmoud El-Kati; Pete and Bud Buckman and friends on the North Shore of Lake Superior where much of the book was written; Diane Adair and her family in Kentucky and Tennessee; James C. Klotter, Kentucky Historical Society; Mr. and Mrs. John Marshall Prewitt, Mount Sterling, Kentucky; Buddy Lubbock, Bernheim Forest Arboretum and Nature Center, Sheperdsville, Kentucky; Jim Holmberg, Filson Club, Louisville, Kentucky; Bill Marshall, University of Kentucky Library, Special Collections; the staff at the Stones River National Battlefield and Cemetery, Murfreesboro, Tennessee; Jan Robinson; Jean and Mitch Charnley; Carol Prafcke; David Noble, University of Minnesota; James D. Layzell (Skip); Joanne and Nat Hart; Cary Waterman; and Paulette Bates Alden. Without their many gifts, this book would not have been written.

CIVIL BLOOD

CIVIL BLOOD

has been set in Bembo Bookface
by Stanton Publication Services, and
is printed on acid-free Glatfelter paper.
The book is published in paper with a
film-laminate finish, and in a cloth edition,
case bound in Van Heek linen at the
Campbell-Logan Bindery. The first
cloth edition of 500 copies is
signed by the author
and the artist.

Jill Breckenridge has taught English, history, and creative as well as business writing; she has edited a newspaper, and been the director of The Loft, a center for writers. Her honors include a Bush Foundation Fellowship, two Minnesota State Arts Board grants, and Loft-McKnight Writers Awards in both poetry and creative prose. Her poems and poem sequences have been published in many magazines. She holds an MFA in Creative Writing from Goddard College, and is completing a Master's Degree in Counseling Psychology with an emphasis on creativity for her work with writers.